Light the Lantern, Daughter

Light the Lantern, Daughter

Ann Cunningham Burke

REVIEW AND HERALD PUBLISHING ASSOCIATION
Washington, DC 20039-0555
Hagerstown, MD 21740

Copyright © 1986 by

Review and Herald Publishing Association

This book was

Edited by Gerald Wheeler

Designed by Richard Steadham

Cover art by Nathan Greene

Type set: 11/12 Tiffany

Printed in U.S.A.

Library of Congress Cataloging in Publication Data

Burke, Ann Cunningham, 1937-
   Light the lantern, daughter.

   1. Thompson, Jenny. 2. Seventh-day Adventists—
United States—Biography. 3. Physical therapists—
United States—Biography. I. Title.
BX6193.T48B87   1986   286.7'32'0924 [B] 86-15412
ISBN 0-8280-0324-6

DEDICATION

To Ken
who made it possible
for me to write this book;
to Mother and Daddy
who stood by faithfully;
and to Tom, Kaye, Sisi, and Danny
who are simply very special.

FOREWORD

Perhaps I could have chronicled my mother's history with exactness, adhering strictly to names, dates, and sequence. This could have been a biography. It is not. I chose to weave Mother's remembrances into a **story,** preferring the flesh and blood of human emotion to the bare bones of fact.

Many of the incidents in this book happened as described. All are based on fact. When I share the story with Mother, she relives her girlhood, which leads me to suspect that, in choosing to imagine, I have come close to catching the way it really was.

—acb

1 The twilight brought a softness to the log house that was not there in the day. That both the house and barns were unpainted and the yard was dirt swept smooth did not seem to matter when the sky turned from pink to gray and the woods across the road grew dark. Katydids started up in the lowland behind the house. In the nearby apple trees sparrows finished their evening songs.

Jenny Thompson stood at the window that looked out on the front porch. Behind her, two large feather beds, two chairs facing a fireplace, and a homemade chest of drawers furnished a room in which the wood floors were scrubbed clean and the clay-daubed walls papered with newspaper. It was not a well-to-do house, but it ranked fair among peers in Cherokee Springs. In the early 1900s the wealth of the flatwoods country of South Carolina consisted of the mineral spring to which people from Spartanburg came for jugs of water, the watermelons that grew on its rich soil, or the bales of cotton that went each winter to the mill.

For a long moment Jenny gazed at the sky, watching dull clouds on the horizon pile up into darkness too early for night. If the girl's face was young, it was also intense, as though at 12 years she already gripped life tight as a tote sack full of cotton. Fear was in her eyes as she turned from the window.

"There's a bad cloud yonder, Ma."

"Is?" Her mother glanced up from the pan of apples she was paring, her voice calm. "Let me see." Setting aside her pan, she shook out her checkered skirt and crossed to her

9

daughter's side, two younger girls at her heels.

Jenny stood close to her as they watched the sky begin to boil like wash water in an iron washpot. Thunder threats grew loud, and the sky flickered.

In those flashes Jenny could see the scrawny rose-bushes that bordered their yard, the shrubs where purple ladyfingers bloomed in spring, and down by the dirt road, the apple tree that marked one corner of the property, and the walnut tree, half destroyed by storm that marked the other. They were eerie in the brightness—those two crooked survivors of many a storm like the one approaching. As darkness stretched over the cotton field, lightning slashed the land somewhere beyond the barns. At the sharp, near outcry of thunder, Jenny started and covered her ears.

"She'll outgrow the fear," Ma had said when her eldest child would retreat to a feather bed during a storm as fast as little Lil and Effie. But Jenny had not. It seemed that her fear grew with her. Even now, as tall as Ma and big enough to make biscuits, she still faced each dark cloud with terror.

"It ain't a-going to get you," Pa would tell her, and his eyes confirmed that he did not understand. With Ma it was different.

"I'll light the lantern, daughter," she would say softly. "That'll help you not to be so scared."

Standing stiffly, Jenny shut her eyes to the lightning as Pa and a rugged youth entered and closed the door against the wind.

"Barely did get Beck to the barn!" Pa spoke more to his wife than the rest of them as he removed his straw hat and brushed back an unruly shock of hair. A small man, he was wiry and strong-looking, with keen blue eyes.

Closing the one window in the room Ma pulled a chair up to it. "Here's your chair, Joe."

Her husband hung his hat on a nail behind the door, then took the chair by the window. The boy sat on the other.

"Cloud's a bad one," Pa said with an official air,

wrinkling his forehead. "Come up fast, too." As he spoke, rain began to drum on the roof and drive against the house. Jenny crawled onto a feather bed and stopped her ears.

"Here's the lantern, daughter." Ma lit a kerosene lantern on the chest of drawers, and her daughter peeked cautiously at its gentle glow before she squeezed her eyes shut against another searing flash of lightning. She loved the old lantern. It was there each time she looked—a safe, homey light, lit by someone who loved her.

At last the flashes came less often, the rain fell more gently, and the thunder only rumbled in the distance.

"Cloud's going around," Pa announced, and Jenny let her breath out.

It was after noon the next day before anyone noticed the big tent going up at Jess Taylor's place. On her way to the field, Jenny spied it. At first she stood transfixed, almost doubting her senses. Then she found her voice. "Lil! Effie! Look yonder!"

Effie stopped tracing in the dirt with her big toe, Lil stood openmouthed, and their half brother Bob pushed his hat back to gaze. Even Pa shaded his eyes against the sun and stared.

"Well, I declare," he said.

Ma knew no more about the large yellow tent than the rest of them. But of course, Pa would know, chatting as he did with the workers who helped him tend Mrs. Acord's farm—Pa whom folks from miles around called to shoot their hogs, who strutted to community singings in a swallow-tail coat and sat barefoot on the front porch Sundays, holding a big family Bible and greeting each churchgoer who passed. Yet he didn't. He vowed he'd find out something, though, and Jenny had no doubt that he would.

News traveled fast in the flatwoods, partly because everyone knew everyone else and partly because there was so little of it. Word of mouth was the vehicle by which it

11

traveled, and a good one, too.

"Talked to Hubert Smith this afternoon," Pa remarked as Ma dished out the cabbage that was simmering on the iron cookstove and placed it with the corn bread on the supper table.

Her face signaled interest. "Did?"

"Yep. Talked to him right smart."

Jenny poked Lil under the table, and Ma seated herself across from her husband, scanning his face.

"It's the Advents," he said. He helped himself to the cabbage and handed the bowl to Bob. "Come in a caravan of wagons."

As Pa talked Jenny watched her mother's plump face. It was a kind face with dark hair pulled back in a bun. Ma raised her eyebrows slightly.

"Advents?" She repeated the word softly so that it didn't sound as bad as when Pa said it. "Advents." Her blue eyes looked puzzled. "What are they, Joe?"

Her husband speared a hunk of boiled cabbage with his fork and held it in midair. "Some religious bunch, I reckon. Ain't nobody knows much about them except they keep Saturday for Sunday and don't eat no pork." His voice put a period at the end of the sentence.

Suddenly he chuckled.

"Want to hear a good one? A bunch of community men heard they was coming and lined up on both sides of the road, aiming to stop them."

Jenny edged closer to the table as her father went on.

"Directly their three wagons come along—and went right on by with nobody saying a word!" He laughed and slapped his leg.

"What happened then, Pa?" Lil's eyes sparkled.

"Well, after the wagons had done passed, the men begun to talk. Old man Jenkins said Adams should have spoke up, and Adams said Jenkins should have, and they all commenced to argue with one another. Finally they broke up and went on home."

As Pa spoke, Jenny pictured the flatwoods farmers in

overalls and straw hats, standing with open mouths as the last wagon rolled past. She laughed until she felt weak all over.

"But how come the tent's in the Taylors' yard, and what do the Advents aim to do here?" Ma asked him when she had finished laughing.

"They pitched one night in the schoolyard. Next day Jenkins and his men come and forbid them to stay." He grinned. "Guess they finally got theirselves a speaker!"

"But the Taylors—" Bob began.

"Jess Taylor come up about then." Pa lowered his voice. "Must have thought they was acting pretty mean for church folks. Looked the Advent preachers over and says, 'You can pitch your tent in my yard just as long as you want to.' So there it is, yonder under them big oaks. Heap better spot than the schoolyard if you ask me!"

Ma still looked puzzled. "But what *do* they aim to do with it, Joe?"

Pa wiped his mouth and pushed his chair from the table. "Have meetings, I reckon. Just have to wait and see."

September was warm as usual. The rosebushes bordering the acre between the house and the mailbox still boasted a few red stragglers. Lightning bugs blinked around the porch in the evening, and in the woods only a few maple leaves had as yet turned yellow. Jenny's thirteenth birthday and the beginning of school arrived together with cotton picking—of the three, the cotton picking ranking first. The cotton was always first. Though Jenny disliked leaving school in April to plant the light-green seeds and missing it again in the fall to pick cotton, it had to be done.

"You're a good picker, Jenny!" Ma often exclaimed, watching her sun-browned hands fly over the cotton plants. And her daughter smiled.

She felt close to her mother—pleasant, easygoing Ma who worked hard for Pa, the girls, and Pa's older children when they were around. How could she be so calm when the girls and their teenage half brother squabbled or Pa lost his temper? Often Jenny thought about it. Ma stood straight and made up her own mind about things, yet she was gentle. To Jenny, she *was* "home."

On the day of the first tent meeting Jenny worked especially fast. Ma said she wanted to see what the preaching was about, and Pa allowed he did too. The family left the field while the sun was a good way above the trees so as to heat water and wash up extra at the tin basin in the kitchen.

By the time they walked the half mile to the Taylors', twilight had descended upon them. The air was fresh on Jenny's face, and under her feet the dirt was barely warm. Ahead, someone lit a lantern in the tent, making it a great yellow jack-o'-lantern. As the girl watched the people entering it, she felt excitement bubbling up inside, livelier than the water at the mineral spring.

"Hurry! Oh, hurry!" she cried, running ahead, and they all quickened their steps.

2 Among neighbors at the tent Jenny spotted the Sutherlands from the next farm up the road. She grinned at yellow-haired Della Sutherland, and the girl grinned back.

Wiggling her toes in the cool grass, she watched the people enter—men in clean overalls and women in fresh skirts and blouses, faces scrubbed and hair smoothed back after working in the field. Children hid behind their mothers' skirts. Young people cast furtive looks at one another, while old folks, halting and wrinkled, shuffled to the front where they would be able to hear better. As they came down the center aisle and found seats Jenny followed them with her eyes.

If they all had one thing in common, it was curiosity—a wondering why this strange big tent now stood in their flatland, their country where everything from crops to calving was familiar, and few surprises like a sudden thundershower shattered the pattern of their lives.

The singing began, a pleasant, middle-aged "Preacher Steel" leading it. It was the singing of people who knew what it was to lose the crop or the mule, or bury a baby in the schoolyard in a pine box. Jenny's strong alto voice rang out beside her mother's clear soprano.

After a "Preacher Sash" welcomed everybody, the meeting began. Clean-shaven "Preacher Brothers" talked of Jesus' return, showing pictures of strange beasts from the book of Daniel and saying that they somehow proved His coming near. Wide awake to the end, Jenny listened, but Lil squirmed and Effie nodded, her bare feet dangling inches from the ground.

"Carry her, Joe," Ma pleaded when the meeting was over, and Pa toted her the half mile home.

They attended every night after that, Ma and the girls. Bob went often, and Pa sometimes. Together they laughed at the postcard that soon appeared in their mailbox. On it three yellow, horned heads accompanied a verse.

"Steel, Brothers, and Sash,
Out of a box, all at a dash!
They ate no meat, only hash.
They paid their debts and spent their cash."

Neighbors received the postcard too. The window of Jenkins' store even displayed one, and people speculated that he was the author-artist. They chuckled about that.

" 'Paid their debts'!" they quoted from the verse. "Well, that's more than Jenkins does!"

After Preacher Brothers spoke about a strange seventh-day Sabbath, Pa did not go back often. Once when he went with Ma and the girls, two of the preachers walked home with them.

"Won't you stay a spell?" Ma invited, smiling, as they reached the house.

Mr. Thompson did not smile, though he offered the men a chair on the porch while his wife hurried the older girls off to get into long nightgowns and helped Effie into hers.

Jenny hoped the preachers did not notice her and Lil slipping into the feather bed near the window. As she scooted under the cool quilts, she left one ear uncovered so she could hear.

"We've been mighty happy to have you all at the meetings, Mr. Thompson!" Brothers began. "You have a fine family! From the prophecies we've been studying, we know it's time to get our families ready to meet the Lord." He paused, and the only sound was the croaking of frogs down at Dugaway Creek. "I notice, Mr. Thompson, that you've missed some of the meetings since we've—uh—spoken about the Sabbath. I—"

"Don't make no matter what day you keep," Pa replied. Jenny grabbed her sister's hand and held it tight.

"I see," Brothers said, clearing his throat. "You remember, Mr. Thompson, that at the end of Creation week God 'blessed the seventh day, and *sanctified* it'?* That means He made it special." The man's voice was calm. "Sounds to me like He wanted us to remember that He made us and all we have—like He wanted us never to forget it. Do you see?"

It seemed to Jenny that even the frogs were quiet.

After a time Ma joined the men, speaking of comfortable things. Lil began to breathe evenly, but Jenny continued to listen.

"Shall we pray together?" Brothers suggested at last. Jenny heard the shuffling of feet and the front legs of Pa's chair hitting the floor. The preachers prayed, and then Ma. In the silence that was her father's turn, Jenny's stomach knotted.

Next morning as she passed the pantry off the kitchen, she saw her mother kneeling by the flour barrel, but at breakfast nobody mentioned the men's visit.

"Wonder why Pa ain't friendlier to the preachers?" Lil asked as she and Jenny carried fodder to the barn. The autumn sun fell kindly on her ruddy farm-girl face.

"He's independent, Lil—just like you!" Jenny jostled her sister good-naturedly, but her eyes were serious.

"What do you mean, *independent?*" Eleven-year-old Lil wrinkled her nose. "If Pa and I are 'independent,' what is it?"

Jenny faced her. "You know how you feel when Pa tells you to get to the house and you don't want to?"

"Yeah."

"Well, that's how Pa feels when the preachers teach something he doesn't want to believe. That's *independent,* Lil."

Saturday morning dawned with Pa out about the barn. By the time the new Sabbathkeepers approached the tent to

* Genesis 2:3.

17

worship, he had taken his plow to the roadside strip of land he seemed to have saved for the occasion, and in their sight he plowed all morning.

The days passed, woven on a loom of time as sturdy and unfailing as the wooden frame on which Ma made dyed cotton stockings that reached past the knees and colored gloves without fingers for picking cotton in the fall. Long before Christmas the tent came down and the Adventist preachers went away, leaving a small group who believed their teaching. Ma was one of them.

She didn't say much about it to Pa that Jenny overheard, only that she had dreamed of two ladders to heaven. On one she and the children climbed. At the foot of the other stood her husband. Mrs. Thompson spoke of the dream quietly, without tears and pleading, but Jenny saw her often in the pantry on her knees and guessed that it was hard to climb alone.

Just when her mother took sick the girl could not tell. At first it seemed only that she tired too soon.

"Going to the house already?" Jenny questioned the first day Ma left the field before the others.

"Yes, daughter, I think I'll go early today." Ma brushed a lock of hair from her face and walked slowly toward the log house. It got to be the same every day. Sometimes she complained that her side hurt.

New Year's night was cold. The two barn cats soft-footed their way in through the kitchen door cathole to stretch out near the hearth. Pa, at his accustomed place near the fire, chewed his wad of tobacco and spat, from time to time, toward the burning log. Ma, too, sat by the fireplace, her hands idle in her lap. Suddenly she turned to the girls.

"Get down off that feather bed and find me the raveled-sock ball." She smiled at Effie whose blue eyes lit up with more than firelight.

After a scramble, Jenny was first to spot the ball. "There it is—under the table yonder!" she squealed, as excited as Effie and Lil in spite of her 13 years.

They plopped down on the floor opposite each other—Jenny and Effie, Lil and Ma. Then Ma rolled the yarn ball across the smooth wood to Jenny who sent it on to Lil who missed Effie by a full foot and rolled it under the bed.

"Can't roll a ball straight! Can't roll a ball straight!" Effie squealed, scooting stomach down to retrieve it. It was a night of warmth and fun, field work forgotten, all the world confined in one familiar, firelit room.

And it was the last night before Ma took to her bed.

More than two months passed before "Miz Eva" Parker from down the road prevailed upon Pa to do something about his wife's condition.

The Parkers were good neighbors even if they *had* adopted what Mr. Thompson considered the foolishness of Sabbath observance. One-eyed "Mr. Mitchell" Parker was well-to-do, having two mules instead of one as most folks had, and Miz Eva did not work in the field.

"Ella ain't doing good, Joe," Jenny heard Mrs. Parker declare one evening in the kitchen. "Appears to me she's weaker."

"Maybe so." Pa stroked his yellow-gray beard. "The resting up ain't helped much yet, but come spring—"

"You better not wait for spring, Joe." Miz Eva looked solemn. "Let us take her on in to the Good Samaritan Hospital in Spartanburg."

A worried expression on his face, he shook his head.

"Joe, there ain't anybody around these parts can help Ella." Miz Eva looked at him pleadingly. "Will you let us take her?"

Pa sighed. "All right. You can take her in the morning." Ma seemed willing to go.

"When a bad cloud comes up, you light the lantern, daughter," she told Jenny that evening. "It'll help you not to be so scared."

"I will," her daughter promised. She thought about the hospital before she went to sleep. The Good Samaritan. Surely they could help her mother there. Still her eyes flooded when, in the morning, Pa and Mr. Mitchell carried Ma to the Parkers' spring wagon for the trip to town.

Ma understood the girl's feelings as usual. "Now, daughter, don't worry. I'll be back." She waved to Pa and the children and was gone.

They visited her once during the three months she was away. The rest of the time, it seemed, they did nothing but work. Jenny rose before dawn to milk and make corn bread or biscuits. She boiled dirty clothes in the three-legged iron washpot and beat them clean on the battling bench. She ironed clothes on the kitchen table. She labored in the field.

The day she learned her mother was coming home, Jenny let out a long, happy sigh. It was not just that she was tired. She wanted *Ma*.

"Ma's coming home! Ma's coming home!" A great surge of energy flowed into her tired body. "Lil! Effie! Pick up the June apples under the trees! I'm going to make a pie!"

Ma smelled it as soon as she arrived. "I smell something good!" she exclaimed as they carried her through the front door to the feather bed.

Jenny beamed. "It's a green-apple pie."

But she noticed that her mother did not come to the supper table. Her face was thin, and she seemed no stronger than before.

A weight heavier than any tote sack settled on the girl's heart.

What was happening to Ma?

Would she *die*?

3 On the fourth day home Ma summoned Pa and Bob from the field. Jenny, Lil, and Effie stood quietly with them as she called each aside. Starting with the littlest, she prayed with them. Effie. Lil. Jenny. Bob. Finally she prayed with Pa.

On the fifth day she died.

Forever Jenny would remember the little churchyard grave where they put Ma the next day, all fixed up in a coffin from Spartanburg. And the empty house after the funeral, with Pa and Bob gone out to plow. She'd remember, too, the words of Mr. Mitchell who looked down at her kindly with his one good eye.

"Your ma was an Adventist, Jenny. She couldn't be baptized because she was sick. But she believed. You're going to see her when Jesus comes!"

It was the longest summer of the girl's life. Mechanically she set the milk to clabber, scrubbed the board floors of the log house, and buttoned 9-year-old Effie's dresses in the back. She could not tell when she missed her mother most. It may have been when, over the little rise in the land people called "the hill," a thunderstorm brewed, and, reaching for the old lantern, she lit it herself.

When the cotton picking ended, she went to school in the small Adventist church half a mile up the road, past the Sutherlands'. Della attended too. It was good to have a best friend beside her on the backless plank bench. With Della she forgot she was "mother" to a family at 13. Grinning and giggling, she felt like a child again.

Winter gave way to buds and quick showers. Mr. Thompson fixed gourds for bluebird houses, made terraces to keep the soil from eroding, and turned the ground for planting corn and cotton.

"I'll never get through the eighth grade!" Jenny moaned to Della the day they both left school. "It's cotton in spring and cotton in the fall with a dab of school between. Here I am—14 and in the third grade!"

"I know." The other girl's blue eyes were serious. "It's the same with me, Jenny." She brightened. "They say girls don't need much education, though."

"Maybe not. Maybe we'll just get married and tend our husbands' cotton fields."

Della tossed her blonde hair. "Maybe *you* will, Jenny Thompson, but *I'm* not going to marry for a long, long time!"

Jenny did not know what she would do without Della. She was almost "family," along with Lil who aimed Pa's gun well enough to shoot a gourd off a fence post, Effie who knew how to gentle her father along, and Bob who teased the life out of Jenny.

"Why do you wash your hands after you make biscuits instead of before, Jen?" His eyes looked so serious when he teased, Jenny never knew at first whether he meant it or not.

"I *did* wash before." She lifted dripping hands from the basin and glared at her big half brother.

"Oh, but I saw you wash them *after*." He leaned against the door frame and eyed her accusingly.

"Git!" Stamping her foot, she flipped water at him, knowing it wouldn't help. At times he stood up for her, though, and a certain closeness developed between them.

"You go on to church," he encouraged one sunny Sabbath when Pa would not let her attend. "I'll stand between you."

Jenny knew what Bob meant. More than once she had jumped between Pa and Ma when Pa was angry. She'd seen her father impatiently hurl an empty salt shaker through the

22

open door, or tear down a chicken coop in rage. "Butter wouldn't melt in his mouth when he ain't mad," Ma used to say.

"Go on," Bob urged.

She went.

Hurrying home after church, she warmed the string beans without humming as she often did. When Pa came from the field at half past twelve, he was quiet too. He took the gourd dipper from its nail, washed his hands over a bucket, and splashed cold water on his face, drying it on his blue shirt sleeve.

"Might come up a cloud directly," Bob observed, puttering nearby.

Pa grunted.

"Reckon it's a bad one?" the boy pursued.

Mr. Thompson squinted at the sky, and Jenny waited for his voice. "Likely not," he said finally, and sat down.

Bob caught her eye. She knew what he was thinking. Either Pa had thought better of the church matter or he sensed that Jenny was not a little girl whose legs he could redden with a switch.

"Reckon you're right, Pa." Bob winked at his half sister. "Likely it'll turn off fair."

Crops went into the ground, grew, and were gathered. Girlhood moved toward womanhood as the dawn toward the day. Jenny worked out in the Parkers' field at a dollar a day for a new dress to match her eyes and made herself a duster cap from which a curl peeked out beside each ear.

On Sabbath she liked to arrive early at the small white church at the edge of the woods. No lack of steeple, stained glass, carpets, and pews could mar the joy of singing at the top of her voice.

"Amazing grace! how sweet the sound,
That saved a wretch like me! . . ."

She watched Rosie Smith's black shoes pumping the

organ and, patting her own foot on the board floor, wished she could play like her.

Mrs. Sutherland's summer roses decorated the rostrum, and Miz Eva and Mr. Mitchell fanned themselves with store-bought paper fans, the morning Elder Simpson from the conference came to preach.

"'Repent, and be baptized,'" he read from his black Bible.* Though he did not shout or shake his finger as some preachers did, his words were solemn. After a verse about being "buried" with Jesus by baptism and "rising" with Him to a new life, he closed his Bible.

"Is there anyone here," he asked, "who wants to be baptized?"

In the quietness Jenny shifted her eyes from his face. Outside the window the leaves of a churchyard oak hung still in the June heat.

"Your ma was an Adventist, Jenny," Mr. Mitchell had said. *"She couldn't be baptized because she was sick . . . "*

"I want to!" Jenny longed to call out. But her voice was silent. She told her half brother about it when she got home.

"I want to be baptized, Bob."

"You do?" He eyed her, it seemed, critically. At 16, did she look as she felt—half child, half grown-up? Not finished, quite, with tossing the ball over the house to Della, yet almost ready for bigger things?

"It's all right," he said at last, as though he were her father. "You go ahead."

Elder Simpson did the baptizing in a dammed-up spot in Dugaway Creek, and Jenny came up out of the cool water and prayed to walk in new life. She was aware, each day after, that now she was a church member. It was a steadying thought. Yet in some disappointing ways she found that she was still Jenny and Pa was still Pa.

She wished she could be close to him. Sometimes on a winter evening, watching him spit toward the fireplace as she picked out cotton from dry, brown burrs, Jenny wondered about him.

"His name ain't really 'Joe,'" her mother had remarked

* Acts 2:38.

once as they swept the dirt yard together. "Name's 'Stephen Elihu.'"

"Why do you call him 'Joe' then, Ma?" Jenny wrinkled her nose in curiosity.

"It's like this." Mrs. Thompson's broom made short, decisive swaths near the doorstep. "When your pa was a boy he had a calf named 'Joe' that his pa slaughtered." Ma paused, and her eyes were gentle. "After that, your pa would never answer to any name but 'Joe.'"

Jenny tried to imagine him without his yellow-gray beard. Pa without a heavy blue work shirt and baggy overalls. Pa as a boy, skinny and barefooted and crying over his calf. Then she thought of him now.

"Never mind the housework. Housework can wait. Field work's got to be done." His face was stern and unsmiling as he ordered her to the field.

It was odd about Pa. He was like a puzzle with pieces hard to fit together. One piece had to do with him once signing a note to become surety for a man and losing his house because of it. One was him working hard to support his first wife and six children. And another was the death of his wife and baby when the seventh was born.

"Your pa made the baby's casket hisself," Ma had told Jenny the story, "and carried it on his shoulder to the church. When the folks there saw him coming, they tolled the church bell forty-one times—once for each year of his first wife's life and once for the baby."

Jenny felt sad when she thought of his hard times. But why couldn't he make things easier for her? Why couldn't he tell her he appreciated her? Didn't he love her? Was she just a field hand to him?

There were many pieces to the puzzle named "Pa," but though she worked with them, Jenny could not get them all to fit.

25

4 The summer Bob took a wagonload of young people to camp meeting in Spartanburg was both wonderful and terrible for Jenny. Wonderful because she and Della went to meetings, slept in a campground tent, heard students tell of "working their way" for a Christian education, and met Jed. Terrible because after a hot trip home and a cooling dip in Dugaway Creek, she came down with the fever.

"Typhoid," the doctor said, furrowing his brow. "Wrap her in wet sheets and give her plenty of water."

Day after day Effie waited on her, cooling her head, bringing her drinks, hoping for the fever to break. Vaguely Jenny heard the voices of neighbors fading in and out.

At last the crisis passed, and she grew strong enough to take the mashed food her sister gave her. One day with Bob's help she sat up, and at the end of six weeks she put her feet on the floor.

"Hurrah for Jen!" Bob encouraged. "In no time you'll be a-courting with what's-his-name from camp meeting!"

Thinking of the letter postmarked "Campobello" in her drawer, she grinned weakly. She could almost hear Jed's quiet voice and see his grin and his big freckled hands.

Then she sobered.

"What would he think of me now—skinny and shaky and my hair fallen out from the fever!"

"Oh, he'd still love you." Lil giggled.

"He'd still think you were pretty," Effie added with a smile.

On the day Jed came, Jenny was up early.

"Sweep the front yard, Effie. You mop the floor, Lil," she ordered, fidgeting with the cap from which some of her own hair, attached inside, hung out around the edges. It was a homespun creation but a heap more sightly than her recently bald head.

"How come you're wearing a hat, Jen?" Lil teased.

"Hush, Lil," Effie reprimanded. "Jen looks nice."

Before the afternoon sun had descended far, Jed arrived in a horse-drawn buggy belonging to his mother. Jenny met him at the edge of the yard. "Howdy, Jenny." The young man looked handsome in white tennis shoes topped by white pants and shirt. With glowing eyes she appraised him as he tied the horse to the hitching post under the walnut tree and gave it the bucket of water she fetched.

"Pa says I have to pull tomatoes this afternoon," she explained, eyeing the white shirt and pants. "You can wait at the house."

"That's all right." His eyes crinkled. "I'll help."

Together they picked tomatoes and milked the cows, and, come evening, they sat on the front porch.

"After Pa died," he told her quietly, "I helped Ma run the farm. It was right hard at first"—he stared at something beyond the field and road—"but I had to do it."

Katydids started up and then the frogs. Sitting on the straight-backed chairs Pa and Ma had always used each evening, only close enough together so that Jed could take her hand, they watched the sun go behind the trees.

In the months that followed, he came as often as his mother could spare the buggy on weekends. Somehow she could work all week and hardly feel tired, just knowing she'd see a familiar horse and buggy stirring up the dust of the road.

"You like Jed right smart, don't you?" Della prodded one Sunday as they chatted on the porch. Cotton picking had begun, and the air felt more mellow than sultry.

"Why do you ask?"

Della's eyes twinkled. "Because you're my best girlfriend, and I need to know!" She grew serious. "It's OK if you do, I reckon. You're 17, and Jed's a good Christian."

Jenny looked quickly at her friend. "How do you know what I want?"

"Because"—Della spoke thoughtfully—"I want that too. I don't want to marry just any old boy down the road."

"Me either. I—I pray about it." She paused shyly. "And something else, too."

"What?"

Jenny lowered her eyes as though half afraid to speak her wish aloud. "Ever since I heard those young folks at camp meeting tell about working their way for a Christian education—"

"Go on."

"I wish *I* could do that."

There. She had said it—had voiced a dream that for a cotton field girl seemed almost absurd. It was nearly dark, but she could see that Della's eyes shone.

"Oh, Jenny," the other girl said softly, "I do too!"

Cotton picking had barely ended when the letter came. Jenny found it in the mailbox one Sabbath after church and reached for it eagerly—Campobello postmark, familiar handwriting, and all.

"Go on in, Lil and Effie," she commanded, wishing to tear the envelope open in private.

The letter began as usual.

"Dearest Jenny," she read, moving her lips to the words, "I've been drafted into the army, and I'm leaving today for Camp Gordon. I will write . . ."

First, disbelief flooded her mind.

No. It wasn't true. Jed would be here anytime now, tying the horse to the hitching post yonder.

Then belief—and oh, the disbelief was better! Blindly Jenny ran to the log house and threw herself on the bed.

That winter she sat on the hard bench at school by day and picked out cotton puffs by night. Like the days, the cotton puffs seemed all alike. Like the nights, there seemed no end of them.

From France Jed sent a bright handkerchief, red-and-yellow-and-blue-flowered. Jenny opened it and held it to her nose, but she could not smell his shaving soap.

The Sabbath she returned from church to find Lil and her clothes gone, Jenny thought her cup of sadness would overflow. "Lil! Oh, Lil!" she cried, knowing almost before investigating that a neighbor boy would be missing, too. Lively Lil! Impetuous child! Although she missed her, she hoped her sister would make a good wife.

Jenny did not forget Jed. His memory lingered with her in the field, on the porch, and under the walnut tree. But his letters were few, the two of them had no "understanding," and a girl needed friends. Sometimes it seemed that only the prospect of a neighborhood party kept her going through the long workweek.

"Seems like I *have* to look forward to something, hon," she whispered to Effie one Saturday night as they combed their hair before the mirror.

"I know, Jen." At 14 Effie was shorter with taffy-colored hair and blue eyes that already drew an admirer or two.

From the direction of the road, sounds of laughter approached the log house, then footsteps fell on the porch. Jenny opened the door.

"Come on in, you all!" she invited, speaking softly.

They entered—half a dozen boys and girls old enough to venture from the home nest, yet unready to build their own. One of the boys grinned shyly at her. "Will your pa let you come?"

She nodded. "He said we could if we worked all week in the field." Then she glanced from the boy to a figure under the quilts, face to the wall, in one of the feather beds. "But you better ask him, Jim."

As the boy's eyes followed her glance, a look of surprise crossed his face.

"Your pa in bed already?" he whispered. "He sick or something?"

Jenny shook her head. "Maybe mad," she whispered back. "Sometimes he don't like us going out. Especially since Lil . . ." They stood watching the still hump under the covers and the shock of dark hair that showed at the top. "Ask him."

"He asleep?"

"No."

The chatter near the door diminished until the room grew quiet. Jim cleared his throat.

"Mr. Thompson, there's a popcorn popping at Sutherlands' tonight. Can the girls go?"

The form on the bed did not move. After a long moment Pa's voice broke the silence. "No, they ain't going."

It was quiet as the visitors left the house and their footsteps receded toward the road. Jenny saw that Effie's lip trembled, and though she was older, her own heart felt heavier than a hundred pounds of cotton.

She turned and left the room. There was no use arguing, no help in crying, but the tears came anyway. Rising at four-thirty every morning, she had milked, made corn bread, and started dinner before going to the field. There she had picked up rocks. When her back grew tired, she had knelt. When her knees were sore, she had squatted. All week she had kept herself going with the thought that, come Saturday night, there'd be popcorn popping—and now she couldn't go.

Anger filled her—and the futility she sensed so often since Ma's death, the feeling that you did the same things over and over every week of your life for nothing but cornmeal to make corn bread and a few cents for dress material.

Finally the girl wiped her eyes. A tiny flame flickered in her mind. It had been there before when, hoeing in the field, she had straightened and looked to the horizon.

There's country beyond the hill, she had dreamed. *Roads and cities and schools. Maybe a school where a cotton field girl could work her way . . .*

But the flame never leaped high, for with Ma gone she

had had little time for dream flames and little hope to fuel them. Now it burst into blaze.

She would go to school—would *have* to go to school! It was the only way out from a life that offered no future.

In the kitchen she picked up the gourd dipper, then, without filling it, turned and walked to the doorway of the room where Pa lay with his face to the wall. Not hesitating lest she should lose her courage, she spoke.

5

"I want to go to school."

Though the house was still before Jenny began, it seemed quieter after. The hump under the quilt stirred a little, for Pa understood that she was not talking about the church school at the edge of the woods. She meant boarding school.

"Do you mean that?" he asked without looking at her.

"Yes, sir," she told the back of his head.

The idea almost made her afraid. How could a girl like her go to school? Perhaps Pa would argue with her. "I need you here, Jenny," he might say. "I can't keep the home together without you." Even if he said it harshly, it would sound good. It would seem that she mattered.

But he did not argue. The next day the farm and household goods went up for sale.

Neighbors from all around came to Joe Thompson's selling-out. They bought the plow, the mule, the feather beds, and even the biscuit pan. Their talk was friendly and matter-of-fact as they purchased the pieces of Jenny's home, one after the other.

At the barn she talked softly to the calf Pa had let her have to feed from a bottle and fatten on dishwater. "I'll have to sell you, too, Daisy. None of us'll be staying on here." She stroked the animal's smooth side. "I reckon Pa will live with one of his first wife's daughters, and Effie'll go wherever I do. Oh, Daisy—" Suddenly her stomach felt strange. By the end of the day there would be no more "home"! She would have cried but for a streak of stubbornness in her. After all, she had asked to go to school.

At the Sutherland house that night, Mrs. Sutherland bustled about in motherly fashion. "Effie, you sleep with the young ones," she directed, "and, Jenny"—she smiled at the girl standing beside her sack of belongings—"you sleep with Della. She ain't been feeling good, but I doubt it's catching. Seems like the strong medicine I soaked her in for a skin ailment mighty near took her strength away!" Then she emptied a drawer in a wooden chest for Jenny and Effie's things and hung their clothes behind the door.

"Sure do thank you for taking us in, Miz Sutherland," Jenny told her awkwardly before bedtime.

The woman laid a hand on her shoulder. "You just run on to bed now, child, and sleep like a baby. The good Lord's going to take care of His own."

The two Thompson girls settled in as best they could at the Sutherlands'. They scrubbed the wide floorboards until they looked white, carried sweet potatoes from the summer kitchen behind the house, and helped Mrs. Sutherland beat the washing on the battling bench. It was as close to home as any place could be—but it was not home. Jenny knew they could not stay there forever. She still dreamed of going to school. But how?

"Father, show us what to do," she prayed, lying awake after Della was asleep. "Is there some way I can go to school?"

On Friday night the family went to young people's meeting at the church, all but Della who seemed too tired.

"Just rest, Della," Jenny encouraged. "You can go to Sabbath school in the morning." She thought the girl looked flushed, but maybe it was just the way the sun streamed through the window on her.

The church felt warm after the walk. As they entered and found places on a plank bench near the stove, Jenny held her hands over her ears to warm them. It was strange how an early spring day turned cold when the sun went down. Like life—changing fast with no warning. Suddenly she felt Effie poking her.

"Who's that yonder, Jen, with the gray beard and glasses?"

Her sister looked up to see a stranger at the front of the room. Plainly dressed, he would hardly have attracted attention most places.

"I don't know, hon," Jenny whispered, staring. "I ain't seen him before."

After the singing and prayer, the man rose and adjusted his spectacles. "I'm Mr. Brannon," he explained, "and my son is the principal of Flat Rock Academy." His eyes roved over the little group of young people with their parents. "You may wonder what that is. Well, I'll tell you. 'Flat Rock' is a little boarding school near Douglasville, Georgia."

If Jenny's mouth dropped open she was not aware of it. She stared dumbly at the man with the gray beard and spectacles. It was as though an angel from heaven had suddenly appeared, saying, "Jenny Thompson, your prayers have come up before God."

"One thousand acres for a school were leased by a wealthy landowner who wished to give young people a chance for a Christian education and a good start in life," the man continued.

Jenny leaned forward. *A school! A little boarding school!* Then she sank back. She had no money but that from the sale of Daisy—perhaps enough for a suitcase and middy dress each for her and Effie. No more for school.

"At Flat Rock," Mr. Brannon went on, "the students live in tent-houses and work on the farm or in the kitchen. I won't try to fool you. It is a struggling little school. Sometimes there is barely enough oil in the cruse or meal in the barrel. But the Lord provides for our needs."

The words echoed in her mind. *A struggling little school . . . barely enough . . . the Lord provides . . .* Why, maybe she could fit into a place like that!

After the meeting she approached Mr. Brannon and looked shyly into his kind face. "I want to come to your school," she said.

The morning Mrs. Sutherland took her and Effie to the train station in Spartanburg was cloudless. Farmers turned their fields for spring planting, and sparrows twittered excitedly around the Sutherlands' front porch.

After Mr. Sutherland lifted two new suitcases onto the wagon, Jenny and Effie climbed in, holding high their new blue middy skirts.

"Goodbye, Della." Jenny's eyes filled at the sight of her friend, pale but smiling as though she had not longed to go to boarding school herself. "Maybe your folks'll let you come later, soon as you're strong again."

The girl's lip trembled only a little. "I hope so," she said. "Oh, I hope so!"

The afternoon sun was starting down the sky when the train rumbled away from the little Douglasville station. Suitcases in hand, Jenny and Effie watched it go.

"We're all by ourselves, Jen."

"I know." From where they stood on the wooden platform, Jenny looked around at uncultivated hills of red clay covered by patchy grass with trees here and there. In the distance cattle grazed, and a line of wild berry bushes ran along the dirt road nearby.

"School's that-a-way. Two miles," the attendant inside directed. He spat tobacco juice into a can near the ticket window.

"Thank you, sir," Jenny said. She shaded her eyes and stared down the clay road. Then she turned to Effie. "The man said that-a-way. Let's go."

Before the first bend in the road, her suitcase grew heavy.

"How far *is* two miles, Jen?" Effie asked, shifting hers from one hand to the other.

"Not far, hon. About like from Sutherlands' to the mill."

Suddenly a man's voice startled Jenny. "Evening, girls! Going far?"

She turned. The young man striding to catch up had

such a friendly face that she answered without hesitating. "To Flat Rock Academy."

"Know the place well." His smile was broad as he reached for both suitcases. "Here. Let me carry these."

The distance passed easily with the newcomer adjusting his gait to that of the girls. Jenny marveled that he could carry two suitcases and keep his shoulders straight!

They chatted of trains and cotton, not pausing until, at the top of a slope, the young man stopped. Nodding toward a blue two-story frame house nearby and a sprinkling of small buildings under some big oaks on the hillside, he flashed his smile. "Here we are. This is Flat Rock!"

Jenny gazed at the small structures, wooden at top and bottom with canvas between. *Tent-houses.* Beyond them at the foot of the slope, two larger buildings also seemed to be part of the school.

Silently the girl absorbed the scene—the spring fields, the warmth of the afternoon sun, shadows lying east of the oaks. Smoke rose from a chimney at the bottom of the hill, and approaching from the other direction, a hay wagon rolled onto the small campus. She heard laughter coming from on top of the hay, and in that moment it seemed that she stepped from a dark cave into sunshine.

At the foot of the hill the girls took their suitcases, thanked the young man, and approached the door of one of the main buildings. Her heart beating fast, Jenny hesitated.

Who would she meet here? What would she say? Would the young people accept two poor girls from the flatwoods?

And what would they think of her—almost 19 and in the fifth grade?

Setting her suitcase down, she wiped her hands on her skirt, then straightened her shoulders and reached for the doorknob.

"Come on, hon," she said to her sister.

6 The door opened into a room containing four dining tables covered with white oilcloth. From the adjoining kitchen, the smell of corn bread wafted past. Afternoon sun slanted through the windows as she and Effie hesitated in the doorway, suitcases in hand, new middy dresses limp and wrinkled.

"Reckon anybody's here?" Effie broke the silence just as a large-framed, strong-looking woman appeared in the kitchen door. A flour-sack apron partly covered her cotton dress.

"Howdy! I'm Miz Grant. Can I help you?"

Jenny's eyes fell on the woman's large, low-heeled shoes. "Yes, ma'am. We've come to work and go to school in the fall. Professor Brannon's expecting us, but he ain't sure when."

"Oh, then you must be the Thompson girls." Mrs. Grant seemed pleased in her plain, practical way. She pulled two chairs from a table. "Set down a spell. I'll get the professor."

The gray-eyed man who returned with her wasted no time. "Hello, girls! I'm Professor Brannon." His hand, closing over Jenny's, was big and rough like a farmer's, and his eyes twinkled. "Now let's see. You're Jenny. Am I right? And you"—he turned to Effie who shyly studied her shoes—"must be Effie. We're proud to have you share what we have at Flat Rock! It may not be fancy, but we have a good time here."

It was true about things not being fancy.

"You may move into a tent-house as soon as there's a

vacancy," the professor assured the girls as he showed them to their room in the nearby building intended to house the sick. "I hope this'll do for now."

Jenny nodded. Except for the big bathtub in the corner, nobody would know it is a bathroom, she mused. It had space for her clothes behind the door, a row of windows that wound outward, and, in one corner, a homemade bed.

"By the way"—the man pointed to the structure in the corner—"one of our students built your bed. Boy named Rob Stanton."

She stared curiously at it. It was not like the feather bed at home, but it had a mattress, pillows, and quilts.

"Thank you, sir," she said at last.

As she and Effie joined the students for supper at an oilcloth-covered table, she felt her face flush with excitement. Hardly tasting the sweet potatoes, corn bread, and milk from the school's dairy, she gazed about her.

"Reckon we'll ever know all these folks, hon?" Her eyes wandered from the girl who served tables to the young man with the strange, long pocket on his shirt and the boy whose laugh filled the room. In the doorway an auburn-haired girl appeared, followed by Professor Brannon and a pretty woman Jenny took to be his wife. The professor's eyes roamed the room until he picked out Jenny and Effie, then he strode to their table.

"Evening, girls! I want you to meet my wife and our daughter, Meg."

Mrs. Brannon smiled, and Meg slipped into an empty chair across from Jenny. She was scarcely older than Effie, Jenny reckoned, though her eyes were as serious as those of an older girl.

After supper the students pulled chairs into a semicircle facing the professor, and they all sang while the young man with the long pocket played an old piano. Then Brannon opened his Bible.

" 'Seest thou a man diligent in his business?' " he read. " 'He shall stand before kings; he shall not stand before mean men.' " * His words came slow and thoughtful, as

* Proverbs 22:29.

38

though he read for meaning instead of ceremony, for himself as much as for the young people gathered about. *"Mean* in this verse means 'insignificant,' " he explained, closing the Bible. "It describes men of low aim and little attainment." His eyes narrowed. "Now here's a promise for every young person in this room! Do you want to be among people who are going somewhere? Our text tells us, 'Be diligent, and you will'!"

Jenny carried the promise with her as she and Effie went to their room. She had never considered herself smart or talented. She was not rich, and sometimes she didn't even feel loved. But the verse didn't mention those things. It just said "diligent." That she could be.

"Oh, Effie, ain't it nice here!" she exclaimed, gingerly letting her weight down on the new bed.

"Yeah," Effie said. But Jenny heard her blowing her nose before she went to sleep.

The weeks flew by. At "women's meeting" every Sunday the girls' tasks were appointed, jobs ranging from preparing breakfast to washing clothes in an iron pot at the spring beyond the pasture. Judging by her first job, Jenny reckoned you proved yourself with grits stuck in the cereal bowls. But she felt satisfied, knowing that each day she worked, her "credit" toward the next school year grew.

"Just think, Effie," she remarked, watching students come down the hill from the blue two-story school building. "In the fall *we'll* be going to school!"

"Uh-huh." Effie did not smile. Her sister noticed that often her eyes had a faraway look, and she said little. When one evening in late spring she sobbed out that she wanted to go home, Jenny was not surprised.

"It's all right, hon." She patted the younger girl's shoulder. "You're only 14 and closer to Pa than I am."

"You come too!" Effie begged, as though longing to gather the family about her. "I don't want to leave you!"

Jenny shook her head. "There's nothing there for me, Effie."

"There's Della, and someday Jed'll be back."

"I know."

"Please, Jenny!"

The older girl stared through the window of their room at the evening sky. The sun was an orange ball over the planted hills, and the breeze was soft, barely rustling the young oak leaves. Soon the tent-houses on the slope would light up one by one, like lightning bugs under the trees, and students would study for examinations. She turned to her sister.

"I don't know how to explain it to you, Effie, but I have to stay here. It ain't because I don't like the folks at home, and it ain't Pa. It's—it's the *life*, Effie. I seem to need something different . . . "

"And I need home."

"Yeah."

Jenny rose to close the curtains at the windows. Quietly she slipped into her nightgown.

"How will you get your fare? Where will you live?"

Effie wiped her eyes. "With Lil and her husband. I wrote her that I was homesick. They say if I'll pick cotton for them, they'll send me fare. Oh, Jen"—her shoulders shook as the tears started again—"you'll write, won't you?"

" 'Course I'll write."

"And come see us?"

"I hope so, hon. Someday when I can afford it."

Before the week was over, Effie's fare arrived, and Rob Stanton took her and Jenny to the Douglasville station in the farm wagon. Jenny waved until the little train was a blur far down the track, then, almost without speaking, rode back to the students and teachers who would have to be "family" and the school that was already "home."

"How's your bed holding up?" Rob made conversation as they rolled onto the school grounds.

A grin appeared on her face like sunlight after a shower. "Sometimes," she answered, mischief in her eye.

He looked puzzled. "What do you mean?"

"I mean that three times in three weeks it fell to the floor!" Laughter rose in her throat. "Want to say you're sorry?"

"Oh, I do!" Rob exclaimed, helping her from the wagon. He laughed too, though his face was quite red.

Jenny missed Effie, and she felt a sinking sensation when students left for the summer, waving and carrying fat suitcases. Only a growing friendship with Meg Brannon helped her through days when a sense of aloneness oppressed her, tempting her to think too fondly of the flatwoods.

"I know a little of how you feel, Jenny," Meg confided one evening after worship as they strolled toward Jenny's room. "Sometimes I feel that way too."

"You do?" She turned to her new friend in surprise. "How could you? This is your home!"

"I just do," Meg answered, and while Jenny could not imagine why, she supposed it was true.

Week by week her Flat Rock "roots" pushed deeper as she drank in the friendliness of the other workers and the soul-restoring love of the professor and his wife.

"Come on home with us, Jenny," they often invited after church on Sabbath. "You're our girl too!" And whenever the professor brought Meg a treat from town, he also had one for Jenny. It was comfortable, having a family to care about her as the Brannons did, and she loved them as only a lonely person can. That is why it hurt so much the day she let them down.

It started with the large bunch of bananas Professor Brannon brought to the kitchen storeroom after a Monday morning trip to town. "I'll just put these here, Jenny," he said, carefully laying them on a shelf near the door. "They ought to be about right for supper."

"Yes, sir." She left the batch of bread dough she was punching down in the kitchen to admire the great bunch of bananas, fat and yellow with hardly a sprinkling of brown. "I'll tell Miz Grant when she comes in."

41

As she worked, rounding dough into loaves, brushing oil on their tops, sliding them into the deep, brick-lined oven the professor had built, she thought about the bananas. Her mouth watered. Only at Christmas did she get fresh fruit in the flatwoods, never in June.

On her way from the oven she stepped again into the storeroom to touch the smooth, yellow skin of the fruit. The faint smell of bananas was sweet.

"I've worked all day in this hot kitchen," she told herself with a speck of self-pity. "I believe—I deserve some bananas!"

Two of them broke off easily. Jenny ate them quickly, and they were in her mouth as sweet as honey. Scarcely, though, had she swallowed the last bite when the bitterness began.

She did not laugh as much as usual either that day or the next. She drudged through her work, picking at the corn bread and ignoring the bananas, then tossed at night and awoke tired. Meg noticed that something was wrong.

"You're quiet, Jenny," she observed, her gray eyes searching the girl's face.

"Don't have to talk all the time, do I?" Jenny countered.

"No, I reckon not."

The quietness between them was like a bridge with nobody crossing over.

"But you're *too* quiet. What's the matter?" Meg tried again.

Jenny brushed her aside. "Oh, nothing—nothing much."

By Friday the weight on her heart was almost more than she could bear. She was a thief—an ungrateful thief—after all the Brannons had done for her. If she confessed, they might not love her anymore, and the light would go out of her life. But if she *didn't* confess, would she have to go on like this forever, weighed down and crushed under a yellow mountain of stolen bananas?

Friday night approached—the high point of the week when, as the Sabbath began, students scooted chairs into the usual semicircle to share experiences and praise the Lord.

"Now who would like to say a word for the Lord?" the professor would ask, smiling. And beginning at one end of the row, everyone would testify in turn. No one would be left out.

How can I testify tonight? The question circled in Jenny's thoughts until her face flushed and her heart beat fast. *How can I? How can I?* She kept her eyes on her work and her thoughts to herself, and by evening she had the answer.

7

"Day is dying in the west;
 Heaven is touching earth with rest . . ."

As she mouthed the words of the hymn, Jenny scanned the half-circle of friends gathered in the dining room—Mrs. Grant in a clean apron, her large brown shoes gleaming; the professor and his wife, handsomer than usual in fresh Sabbath clothes; and Meg, next to Jenny as always, auburn curls shining. Down the row were Tim Henson, the young farm manager who made his own shirts, each with a long pocket; Rachel Martin, soon to finish tenth grade and go on to a school they called "Southern Junior College" in Tennessee; Jefferson Jones, of the hearty laugh; Wilton Brown, ruddy-faced from field work; and Seth Retzler, the young Bible teacher just out of the army. The summer group was small and close-knit, yet the closeness did not warm her heart this June evening. She sat stiff and still through the Bible reading as the sun sank behind the Georgia hills and Sabbath came to the little school.

"I'd like to thank the Lord for letting me work at a Christian school," Seth began, his honest blue eyes shining. "I want to serve Him wherever He can use me." He sat down, and, next to him, Wilton stood.

"I learned something in the field this week," Wilton drawled. "It takes work to grow peas, but weeds grow easy!" Jefferson chuckled, and Wilton went on. "I want to cultivate good habits in my life, and not let just anything grow!"

44

"Amen!" The professor smiled as Wilton took his seat.

It seemed to Jenny that as each person rose and sat down, her heart beat a little faster. By the time Meg's turn came, she could not even hear what the girl said. She knew only that she was next.

Almost before Meg was back in her seat, Jenny was on her feet, her hands like ice and her face burning. Without taking time to think of all the eyes upon her, she blurted it out.

"I took two bananas."

Then she sat down. For a moment all was quiet. In disgrace Jenny stared at her lap. Then she heard the professor's voice.

"Thank you for that testimony, Jenny," he said softly. " 'Though your sins be as scarlet, they shall be as white as snow.' " * He sounded kind, but she did not dare to look up until almost time for the closing prayer. When she did, Meg was smiling at her, and Jenny knew that in heaven and on earth she was forgiven.

The tent-house she moved into that summer was pure joy to her. With the delight of sparrows gathering twigs in spring, she and Meg brought her belongings from the bathroom to her new home--one room, large enough for two cots, a chest, and a little woodburning stove.

"Wish you could live here with me, Meg!" She voiced her thoughts as she made up the cot of her choice.

"Me too!" The other girl rolled up the canvas on one side of the room to let in the morning sunshine. "This is so nice—in a rough sort of way!"

"I know. And I don't mind 'roughing it.' I grew up doing that."

Meg turned to her friend with interest. "Tell me about your home, Jenny. You never have."

"Reckon I haven't."

"Well, do! I want to know about it."

Jenny gazed through the tent-house "window" at the wide pasture with its sprinkling of brown and white cows.

* Isaiah 1:18.

45

"It was a log house, Meg. Not near as nice as your place. But Ma kept things right nice when she was alive." Jenny paused, remembering. "It was a good home with Ma there."

"Your ma must have been nice."

"She was a good woman."

"You still miss her, don't you?"

"I'll *always* miss my ma."

The tent-house was suddenly quiet. Only the distant voice of Jefferson Jones calling to the farm mule broke the stillness. When Meg spoke again, it was very softly. "I never saw my ma."

Jenny's forehead wrinkled. She spun to face her friend. "You never saw your ma? I don't know what you're talking about."

Meg looked as solemn as Jenny had ever seen her. "Jenny, I'm adopted."

"You ain't. But, Meg—you *belong* to the professor—I mean—you couldn't have a better—"

"I know."

The other girl grew quiet again. Jenny touched her shoulder. "Does it bother you, Meg?"

Suddenly the gray eyes filled with tears. "I don't know why it does, Jenny. I don't know why!"

"But it still does, don't it?"

"Yes. Sometimes at night I slip outside and sit on the back steps and cry."

"Oh, Meg!" Jenny gazed across the pasture to the place where new corn was finding the sun. "And I reckon I thought *I* was the only lonely one in the world!"

"Yeah." Meg smiled at that. "Maybe I did too."

Autumn brought almost too much excitement for Jenny—new students arriving timidly, old ones returning with wide grins and hugs, and, coming to share the tent-house, a roommate!

"I'm just thrilled to be here!" Juanita bustled about the room, adding personal touches. "This quilt is from my grandma, the lantern's Pa's, and Ma made the braided rug . . ."

46

Smiling, scarcely keeping up with the flow of information but not minding much, Jenny watched her. Here was a roommate—her first since Effie. She scrutinized the plump girl from dark hair and freckles to black buttoned shoes, and decided she would "pass." She would not take Meg's place, of course. But Jenny enjoyed friends as she did songs, some for the words and some for the music. This one—she chuckled as she watched Juanita bounce about—she'd enjoy for the rhythm!

Word from Effie both brightened and saddened Jenny's life. Bob was marrying a girl named Amy Jones and moving to Spartanburg; Effie was seeing a farm boy, Fillman Ross, and liking it; and Della was worse.

"Oh, no, Della!" Jenny said aloud when she read the diagnosis. Tuberculosis! Hardly anybody got well from that.

Letters from Jed sought her out as well. He was her only link with a war that seemed as far from the Georgia hills as it had from the cotton field. Vaguely she understood that nations fought each other over power and territory, but the only thing she really grasped was that Jed who had once tied his ma's horse under the walnut tree had stopped coming. That was war. She hated it.

Rumors of peace talks circulated, sifting through to the little school to be discussed at mealtime and prayed over at worship. Jenny listened with more interest than she cared to advertise.

If the war should end and Jed should come home, what then? Would he still like her? Would she still like him? Mentally she numbered the "good Christian boys" she knew. Tim. Jefferson. Wilton. They were fine boys, no question about it. But in her heart she knew nobody rivaled him.

She was working in the kitchen on the November afternoon that the news arrived. Bent routinely over a dishpanful of bread dough, she suddenly became aware of a commotion on the hillside. Quickly stepping to the window, she saw Juanita shouting and leaping through the dry stalks that remained of the school's cotton crop.

With her mouth open, Jenny watched the girl's descent.

"Your silk stockings—" she began as the door burst open and her roommate stood panting before her. "You've torn—"

But Juanita's glowing face silenced her.

"Jenny! Jenny!" she burst out. "The war is over!"

"Jed will be home one of these days," Jenny wrote to Effie that night by lantern light. "Reckon I'll ever get to see him? Tell Lil hello for me—and Della. Poor Della! I can't believe it, Effie! I miss you all. Love, Jenny."

She wondered when she would see them all again, and a lump rose in her throat. It was one thing to leave home in a burst of independence and quite another to pass long months without the sight of it. Turning her face from Juanita, she scooted under the quilts and pretended to sleep.

Some of the students went home for Thanksgiving and most for Christmas. With a sinking feeling, Jenny watched them go. "Never mind, Jenny. We'll have fun," Meg comforted.

Jenny swallowed hard. "Yeah," she said.

One afternoon before Christmas Mrs. Grant sent her to the stockroom in the basement of the schoolhouse.

"Bring down some sweet potatoes for the storeroom here," she instructed, "and some of those dry cowpeas." She reached for a sack. "Here. Take this."

"Yes, ma'am." Jenny slipped into her coat and turned the collar up. Gray clouds shut out the sun, and the wind was raw. She thrust her free hand deep into her coat pocket as she climbed.

At the stockroom door the faint, earthy smell of produce greeted her. Inside, the professor and Tim Henson unloaded provisions from town. As her eyes grew accustomed to the dim light, Jenny noticed the large bunch of bananas Brannon pulled from a gunny sack.

"I got us a treat in town." His eyes twinkled as he held

48

up the bunch of bananas.

She looked at them. They were fat and yellow with not the least sprinkling of brown.

"These should keep a day or so if we put them here where it's cool," the professor continued, laying them on a shelf. Memory burned her face as he caught her eye.

"Yes, sir." She noticed that he broke two of the fattest ones from the bunch. Suddenly he strode toward her and stuffed them into her coat pocket.

"Your besetting sin," he said, grinning like a schoolboy.

Jenny giggled. It was hard to stay homesick around a man like that.

The year moved on, classes and work becoming the familiar pattern of her life. Though the goal of tenth-grade graduation from Flat Rock seemed as remote as the evening star over the pasture, she no longer worried about being 19 in the fifth grade. Noticing that one new student even had graying hair, she decided that nobody was too old to go to school, and a person never needed to be ashamed to learn.

"Seest thou a man diligent in his business?" she reminded herself. "He shall stand before kings"! The words became a sort of "lantern" to her, a comfort when arithmetic was hard or black-eyed peas stuck in the cooking pot; when she had no money for stockings or when, with a pang, the question came to her, *Where in this world am I going all alone?*

In early June Jenny heard from Bob. "Ain't it time you took a couple weeks off?" she read his scrawl. "You come see me and Amy, and I'll take you out to Cherokee." Her grin widened as she read the last line. "If you'll come, I'll send money for fare."

She went, of course, wishing the train on toward Spartanburg at a pace it never traveled and waiting for a glimpse of Bob and Amy at the station.

They were there, right beside his wagon, straining for a glimpse of her.

"Welcome home, Jen!" Bob patted her shoulder as he

took her suitcase. "We're proud you're here!" Amy smiled and nodded while Bob looked his half sister up and down. "Don't look like that school done you no harm," he observed lightly, but Jenny knew he meant it.

She laughed happily. "It's a mighty good school, Bob."

Next morning he drove the eight miles into Cherokee Springs as soon as breakfast was over. Jenny's joy mixed with tears as the wagon rumbled into the community, past the schoolyard and the log house, Pa miles away at his daughter's place.

"Take me to Lil's," Jenny directed after she wiped her eyes. "I want to see her and Effie."

They were scarcely more grown up than she remembered, and Jenny thought she could never tire of the sight of them, chatting around Lil's table and vying to tell all the news.

"You remember Fillman, Jen?" Effie put in shyly as soon as it seemed proper. Jenny noted her pink cheeks and assessed the situation in a moment.

"Effie, you're in love!"

The girl giggled. "How can you tell?"

"Takes one to know one!" Lil declared, and it was Jenny's turn for pink cheeks.

"You all hush!" she defended herself. "I ain't found anyone new."

"Anyone *new*," Lil shot back, and Jenny's blush deepened.

"Ain't seen Jed for over a year if that's what you mean." She shook her curls decisively. Then her look softened. "Tell me about Della. How bad off is she?"

"Not too good, Jen." Effie shook her head. "But maybe she'll do better now it's summer."

"If you want me to, I'll take you to Sutherlands' this afternoon," Bob offered, bowing, from the doorway. "At your service, ma'am."

Jenny smiled at his effort to brighten the sad spot in her visit. But though Lil prepared her best biscuits and gravy for the noon meal, she could not get Della off her mind.

50

8 At the front door Mrs. Sutherland hugged Jenny warmly. Her face was worn, but she smiled as she drew the girl inside. "My but it's good to lay eyes on you again! Della talks about you right smart. She's in bed yonder."

Jenny followed the woman to the feather bed in the corner where, from the pillow, a thin face looked up at her.

"Why, Jenny!" Della's voice was soft.

"Della!" Jenny hoped she did not show surprise at the frail shadow of the girl who, with blonde hair shining in the sun, had run and laughed with her. Could this be . . . ? She looked into the blue eyes, and they were the same.

"Sit down." Della patted a spot beside her on the bed. "How is school?"

"It ain't a fancy school," Jenny said, "but it's a good one." She told of the tent-houses, Juanita, the professor, and Meg, watching Della's face for any sign of sadness. But in the eager blue eyes she saw no jealousy, and at the story of the bananas the sick girl chuckled aloud.

"It sounds nice, Jenny!" she said. Then the coughing seized her, shaking her thin shoulders with a vengeance.

"She don't have much strength," Mrs. Sutherland explained when her daughter lay quiet again. "Seems like the coughing wears her plum out."

"I'd better go." Jenny patted the girl's thin hand. "I'll be back."

Several times during the two weeks she visited Bob, she did return, and though the visits made her sad, she hated to end them.

It was a changing world. Jenny knew it in the pit of her stomach when she rode past the log house, when she looked at Della's thin face, and when one day Effie and Fillman appeared at Bob's front door with the announcement "Guess what! We're married!"

The train ride back to school gave her time to sort it all out. Nothing was the same. Not home, not Della, not even Effie.

"I'll remember it the way it was," she mused, staring idly at hills and woods through the train window, "with Ma in the log house making biscuits, and Lil and Effie and me hanging our bare feet over the edge of the porch." A lump formed in her throat. Life moved along like a train, the scenery changing, and you couldn't stop it. You had to move on too.

Something like fear stabbed at her heart—fear of leaving the familiar for the unknown. She wanted to go back to childhood, hurt and all—she did not want to go into the future all alone!

Dimly in the back of her mind something flickered.

"Seest thou a man diligent in his business . . ." Corn fields flashed by, cotton patches, and weathered shanties. The day was clear, like the morning she and Effie first rode the train to Douglasville.

Suddenly Jenny straightened in her seat, her eyes brightening. Why, she had a *promise!* Although she'd always cherish the past, a girl could not go forward while looking back.

The conductor entering the car tipped his hat to her. "Help you with anything, ma'am?"

"No, thanks." Jenny smiled up at him. "Just—could you tell me how far it is to Douglasville?"

She had been back at Flat Rock only two weeks when the letter from Effie came. Della was dead.

With reddened eyes Jenny made bread in the kitchen, mechanically adding flour and kneading it long and hard.

Della. Gone like Ma. She could not believe it, and yet she cried—cried for Della and the girl's mother and herself, and then as she turned and pummeled the great ball of dough, it seemed she cried for the whole world.

"Della wanted to go away to school," she told Meg that evening as they walked slowly toward Jenny's tent-house. "We both did. I got to, and she"—her voice cracked and she went on brokenly—"she couldn't."

"I know."

"*Why*, Meg?"

Her friend shook her head.

Finally Jenny wiped her eyes. "Della was a real Christian," she said. "Meg, I think Della and Ma will both rise from their graves when Jesus comes."

Meg's eyes were bright with sympathetic tears. "Yes, Jenny! Think about that. When you go to bed tonight, think about the resurrection. Promise?"

"I'll try." Before she crawled into her cot, she took a Bible from the little chest and, with Juanita's help, found the verses she needed.

> "For the Lord himself shall descend from heaven with a shout, with the voice of the archangel, and with the trump of God: and the dead in Christ shall rise first: Then we which are alive and remain shall be caught up together with them in the clouds, to meet the Lord in the air: and so shall we ever be with the Lord." *

She read the words twice. At last she spoke. "Juanita, I don't see how a person can *live* without hope!"

Summer mellowed in Georgia, the cotton beginning to fill out the burrs, and late peas all but ready to pick. Early afternoon sun hung over the hillside, and in the school kitchen, heat shimmered off the big iron cookstove.

Moving quickly, Jenny wiped clean the white oilcloth on the dining room tables and swept corn-bread crumbs

* 1 Thessalonians 4:16, 17.

from the floor. From time to time she glanced toward the doorway where flies buzzed around the screen.

"Oh, there you are!" she exclaimed as Meg appeared, auburn curls damp about her face. She swished the broom at the last of the crumbs. "My, child, you're about to roast!"

"Mighty near!" the other girl agreed, wiping her forehead.

Jenny untied her flour-sack apron and hung it on a hook in the kitchen. "'Bye, Miz Grant," she called to the woman stirring flour in the gravy pan. "I finished my job. We're going down to the flat rock."

Mrs. Grant turned. "Have fun!" She lifted her apron to fan her pink face. "You deserve an afternoon off!"

"It's a wonder she'd say that," Jenny whispered as the girls went out the door.

"How come?"

Jenny giggled. "You mean your pa didn't tell you about the molasses—how I left the plug out of the barrel and let half a gallon run onto the floor?"

Meg gasped. "Jenny! How'd you ever get it cleaned up?"

"Your pa's shovel. And then there was that big batch of cottage cheese Juanita and I ruined the other day—"

"No fooling?"

"Just got busy fixing breakfast and let the milk sit too long . . . You should have seen it!"

"So what'd you do?" Meg asked, shaking her head.

"Put it in the old hollow tree out by the spring. Carried it in my apron."

"Jenny, you do beat all!" Meg snickered. "Did you get caught?"

The older girl grinned sheepishly. "Right off. When Tim Henson came in from taking care of the cows, he said, 'What are those two white trails out to the hollow tree?' And I said, 'What white trails?' And then I looked."

"Yeah?"

"Sure enough, two white lines went from the kitchen door across the pasture! I reckon it leaked out both sides of my apron."

" 'Be sure your sin will find you out'!" Meg quoted, chuckling.*

Jenny nodded. "Yep. I know!"

The shade was pleasant on the wooded slope beyond the spring. "Let's take off our shoes and stockings," Jenny suggested as the girls neared a large, slanting rock barely submerged in spring water.

"And slide!" Meg cried, lifting her skirt high and sitting down on the cold, slippery rock. Lively as otters and almost as carefree, they slid down it again and again. Then, shoes and stockings in hand, they strolled back through the pasture.

"That was fun!" Jenny sighed happily. "I feel about 9 years old instead of 19!"

"Nineteen!" Meg glanced appraisingly at her friend. "Why, you're about old enough for Tim!"

Jenny poked the younger girl in the ribs. "You hush, Meg Brannon. You know I could never like Tim."

"Why not?"

"Oh"—she tried to keep her face solemn—"because I can't make shirts with proper pockets."

Meg giggled. "Maybe Seth, then," she pursued.

"Go on! Do I have to get a boyfriend just because both my little sisters are married?"

Suddenly Meg's grin faded. "You're serious, aren't you? When you're 19, do you really wonder what you're going to do with your life? Does it worry you?"

Jenny looked sober. "All I can say is, it's a good thing I'm not graduating next spring like Juanita. 'Cause when I leave Flat Rock, I don't know *where* I'll go."

*Numbers 32:23.

9 The skies of September were splendid. While the maple leaves in the woods turned yellow, the students gathered the crops—corn for the mill, cowpeas for drying, and sweet potatoes for the cool storeroom. It seemed to Jenny that the very hills skipped and sang. If the return of students was merely a cycle repeating—old as schoolteachers and predictable as young people moving up—she did not feel it. She ran to the kitchen window each time she heard the rattle of the farm wagon bringing students from the station in Douglasville, and as she watched the new ones appear timidly at the dining-room door, she remembered her first day at Flat Rock.

"Did I ever tell you about the young man who carried our suitcases, Meg?" she whispered before the professor read the Scripture portion the first evening of the school year.

"Whose suitcases?" Meg's eyes roved the room.

"Mine and Effie's. I never told you about that?"

"No. Tell me."

Jenny glanced at the professor to be sure she had time. "We were walking from the train station when a young man came up and asked us where we were going."

"Uh-huh?"

"We said, 'Flat Rock,' and you know what?"

"What?"

"He carried our suitcases all the way!"

Meg raised her eyebrows. "For two miles? Who was he?"

Jenny shook her head. "That's what I want to know! It's

56

odd. You know, I've never seen him since."

Days hurried by faster than you could run from the schoolhouse to the dining room. Dry leaves scrunched underfoot, and the young people fastened the tent-house flaps securely to keep out the chill. On Sundays the whole student body rode in the farm wagon to nearby Dog River to gather sappy pine knots for starting fires. Jenny and Juanita stacked their supply under the floor to keep it dry.

"Wish I could build a fire good as you!" Juanita exclaimed as Jenny arranged a handful of knots under large sticks in the tent-house stove.

"Never mind, Juanita. You leave this job for me! Remember the day I came from the kitchen to find you with a fire that mighty near blew up the stove? Takes experience to build a good fire."

Her roommate propped her hands on her hips indignantly. "Experience! And how shall I *get* experience?" She rolled her blue eyes. "But never mind. You build the fires. I'm honored to live with such talent."

Jenny laughed. "Speaking of talent, have you ever thought of acting?"

"Don't reckon they do much with that sort of talent at Southern Junior where I'm going, do you?" Juanita grinned amiably. Little flames leaped from the pine knots and wrapped themselves around the sticks. Jenny adjusted the pile.

"Juanita," she said, teasing gone from her voice. "You're lucky."

"Lucky?"

"Yeah. Going to another Christian school when you finish here. It must be nice to have folks."

Juanita studied her face. "You want to go to Southern Junior?"

Jenny shrugged. "I don't know. I want to do something with my life, but I don't have any money, and—well—I'm just a cotton field girl."

"Jenny!" Juanita slipped her arm around her roommate's shoulder. "You aren't 'just a cotton field girl'—you're the only Jenny Thompson in the world!"

Smiling halfheartedly, Jenny replied, "Maybe it's a good thing."

"Don't say that! Didn't the Lord work it out for you to come here? Didn't you tell me that yourself?"

"Well—"

"You did. You know you did! So you're special. See?"

Jenny's smile broadened. "All right. You've made your point."

For evening worship the professor chose a verse Jenny had never heard. Snuggling under an old patchwork quilt that night, she ran it through her mind. *"When my father and my mother forsake me, then the Lord will take me up."* *

Winter was mild by most standards with only one light snow that fell magnificently, making a Christmas card scene of the pasture. Most days were warm enough that Jenny did not miss owning gloves or mind too much that the soles of her shoes were thin. Even so, she was grateful for the extra quilt the professor's wife gave her and felt glad when her morning work kept her near the cookstove.

Time marched by, a rhythmic procession of work, class, study, and sleep. Days ran into months, and months into a school year. Suddenly it was spring. That spring Effie was expecting her first child, and Jenny got the letter from Jed.

"I'd be proud to see you again, Jenny. Seems like ten years since I hitched Ma's horse under your pa's walnut tree, but I reckon it's been just two. If you ever come to Bob's place in Spartanburg, I reckon I could . . ."

Sitting on her bed, she read the letter, once hastily and once slowly. Then she let it fall to her lap and stared unseeing at the board floor of the tent-house. A little smile played at the corners of her mouth. It did seem like ten years! Her feeling for Jed was not as intense as it had been on that Sabbath when she threw herself across the feather bed at home and cried. Time and distance had done their

* Psalm 27:10.

work. All the same . . .

Going to the chest, she opened a drawer and took out paper and pencil. Then she plopped back down on the new quilt and laid the paper on a book in her lap.

"Dear Bob," she began.

Jenny did not think about the coming visit with Jed all the time. She had arithmetic to figure, bread to bake, and clothes to wash and iron often because they were few. Duty filled her life as it always had, but her eyes sparkled and she laughed easily. Mrs. Grant noticed.

"You're right lively," the woman commented one morning as she set a pan of milk to clabber on the back of the cookstove. "Spring affect you that-a-way?"

Jenny chuckled. "Maybe so," she said brightly. "Or maybe it's 'cause I get to go home for a weekend pretty soon."

"Oh!" Mrs. Grant nodded approvingly. "So that's it." She washed her large hands in a basin near the stove and dried them on her flour-sack apron. "I'm right glad for you. Everybody needs a break now and again."

Jenny watched her move about the kitchen. Such a strong, dependable woman! Did people like Mrs. Grant remember about boyfriends? Jenny was not sure. She decided not to mention Jed.

"You'll see your pa this time when you go home, won't you, Jenny?" Meg questioned as they sat on a log near the flat rock one afternoon early in May. New leaves fluttered on the oaks. The pasture grass was greening.

"I reckon."

"He'll be glad." Meg glanced tentatively at her best friend.

"I don't know." Jenny shook her head. "I don't know whether he will or not."

The water running over the flat rock shone silver in the sun. One crow and then two cawed over the pasture. When Meg did not comment, Jenny went on. "I've just never been close to my pa."

Meg nodded. "I figured. Are you mad at him?"

"Well, maybe not—but I still remember some things I don't like." She wrinkled her brow thoughtfully. "The Bible says to honor your parents. I don't know *how* to honor Pa. He used to treat Ma mean, Meg. He had such a temper!"

"I reckon it would be hard. I've always—"

"Oh, it is! I—I don't see how I can!"

The girls sat silently, undisturbed by the raucous cawing of the crows. At last Meg spoke. "Jenny, the Bible doesn't say to honor everything your parents *do.*"

Jenny cocked her head and looked sideways at her. "H'mmm," she said, creasing her forehead. "Reckon it doesn't."

It was that same spring that Jefferson and Wilton, impatient of school rules, ran away. They were back at breakfast next morning, though, after the professor uncannily ran into them in a boxcar at the Douglasville station.

Also that spring Juanita graduated from tenth grade in a ceremony on the schoolhouse lawn.

And it was the spring that Jenny took the money Bob sent and boarded the train for Spartanburg as soon as school was over.

"That's a mighty nice bunch of bananas you've got there!" Meg exclaimed as she told her Goodbye. "Who are they for?"

Jenny grinned shyly. "Pa," she said.

10 The Carolina countryside looked good to Jenny's home-starved eyes. Peach trees grew heavy with little green peaches. Among rows of young cotton plants laid out straight as a man can drive a mule, field hands in bright clothes and straw hats bent over their hoes. Near a weathered shack Jenny glimpsed a family of them—three children, a mother, and a father. Nostalgia and pity filled her.

She even enjoyed seeing Spartanburg. In this center of crowded buildings and paved streets, she had visited Ma at The Good Samaritan Hospital, gone to camp meeting with Della, and first met Jed. Memories swirled in her head as she visited with Bob (now father of two little girls), Lil with a toddler on her hip, Effie waiting for her baby, and Pa sitting straight and gray-bearded in a rocker at Effie's house. She seemed to see Lil shooting gourds off a post with Pa's gun, Effie begging for a biscuit from Ma's black pocketbook, or Pa terracing the place out around the apple trees. But she only smiled and said things such as "He's a pretty boy, Lil," or "Here, Pa. These bananas come from Flat Rock. There we eat them right smart."

Anticipation ran in Jenny's veins all week. Come Sabbath she would see Jed! She imagined him driving his mother's buggy up Pendleton Street and tying the horse to a hitching post near Bob's house. The rest she imagined different ways—him slipping up on her in the kitchen . . . her sitting on the front step when he came . . . By Friday she felt a twinge of fear. How would she act? What would she say? What if he didn't like her anymore?

Or what if he liked her too much? Jenny thought of her Christian education, just beginning. Could she give it all up for him?

When he arrived on Sabbath afternoon, she met him at the door.

"Howdy, Jenny." There was the wide smile she remembered, the gray eyes, the big freckled hands.

"Howdy, Jed. Won't you come on in?"

They sat in straight wooden chairs in Bob's front room, she glancing shyly at him in his blue suit. She had never seen him look so stylish. It was hard to talk at first. The two laughed nervously at Bob's little Annamae and Beth who ran diapered past them in a burst of courage.

The walk to the park was better.

"Yonder's town and the statue of General Morgan on his horse." Jenny pointed down the sidewalk past the row of close, wooden houses. "The park's that-a-way."

They found a bench under a cluster of maples and sat where the grass was green and sun-dappled. "How was the Army?" Jenny questioned.

Jed seemed glad to talk about it. "War's plumb rotten." He shifted his position so as to see her better. "But the Army—well, it helps you grow up, I reckon."

Jed *had* grown up. He had a maturity about him that Jenny had not seen before. She liked it, in a way. Yet in another way it made her uneasy.

"But I'm glad I'm out," he went on, cocking his head and squinting up through the maples. "I like construction work. Been promoted to supervisor already."

"That's nice." She could not think of much to tell about her life. Would she talk about sixth-grade schoolwork? Making bread? It all sounded so plain! Jed would not understand how wonderful Flat Rock was to her, and that she was happier there than she had been since Ma died. When he tried to pull her close to him, she held back.

"Not now, Jed." She did not know how to explain that to her a kiss was special, an acknowledgment she was not ready to make. Someday, maybe, but not yet.

At a quarter till five Jed pulled a gold watch from his pocket and glanced at it. Again at five he looked at the watch. "I'd better be going," he announced.

At the hitching post Jenny petted the horse while he went inside to tell Bob and Amy Goodbye.

"It was good to see you, Jenny," he said softly when he returned to untie the reins from the post. "I'd be proud if you'd write to me."

She smiled up at him. "All right," she answered.

As the sun went down and the first stars appeared above the city, she relived the afternoon from the time she opened the front door for him until she watched his mother's buggy clatter down Pendleton Street and turn the corner.

Yes. She would write. But she wondered . . . why did he have to hurry off? Why couldn't he have stayed for the evening? When she mentioned it to Bob next morning at breakfast, he looked at her strangely.

"You want to know how come he left so soon?"

"How come?"

Bob studied something out the window. "It was payday for the construction workers. He went to pay his men."

Her mouth opened and closed again, and she stared blankly at her half brother. Then the words came.

"On *Sabbath*?"

"I reckon."

Jenny said no more. She ate a helping of grits and excused herself from the table.

Only one person sat near her on the train ride back to Douglasville—a balding man who dozed much of the way, his head nodding to one side and the other. Jenny turned from watching him to the window.

Jed *did* like her too much. She had seen it on his face as they sat beneath the maples and felt it when he tried to pull her to him. Old enough now, and with a good job, he would be looking for a girl to marry.

"I can't marry Jed." Jenny silently formed the words

with her lips. "I can't." Two things she had prayed for—a Christian education and a good Christian man. The first part of that prayer was coming true. And the second part . . . Well, maybe he was not the one.

Her mind turned to the professor, leading as everyone repeated the fourth commandment as the sun went down on Friday evening.

"Six days shalt thou labour, and do all thy work . . ." *

She remembered the peace that filled the room as young voices sang together.

> *"Day is dying in the west;*
> *Heaven is touching earth with rest . . ."*

And she thought of Jed, checking his gold watch and hurrying off to pay his men on Sabbath.

"It won't work, won't work, won't work," the train wheels clacked as they hurried her home to Flat Rock.

Almost as soon as she arrived, Jenny wrote the letter. It was kind but decisive. "Dear Jed, I think it will be better for us to go our separate ways. I'll be in school for a long time yet . . ."

"We don't think alike," she explained to Meg as they lingered at the table after supper. "And I can't give up my school."

"Is it awful hard?" The other girl's face showed her concern. "Breaking up, I mean?"

Jenny shrugged. "At one time it would have been. I felt awful bad when Jed went into the Army." Idly she traced a pattern on the white oilcloth. "Back then I might have married him. Maybe I've been spared."

How the summer flew so fast Jenny could never tell. In the cool of the mornings, students fanned out over the countryside to pick wild blackberries. Bucket in hand she visited the berry bushes, gathering their juicy fruit with the speed of a farm girl. By the time berry season had ended, she had picked forty-five gallons.

* Exodus 20:9.

"Think you're something, picking all those berries!" Rob teased as they carried their buckets to Mrs. Grant.

"Just jealous 'cause you can't pick as fast as I can!" Jenny peered into his half-filled bucket. Rob was like a brother to her—one part mischief and two parts friend. "Where are you going?" she questioned as he hurried off.

"Oh"—he chuckled self-consciously—"I'm going hunting."

"Hunting?"

He chuckled again. "Yep. Skunk hunting."

"You're fooling me, Rob!" She eyed him suspiciously.

"No, I'm not. I learned how years ago." He stretched as tall as he could. "I can get them without getting sprayed."

Doubled over in laughter, she managed, "My, my, Rob! I declare!"

Summer afternoons were hot as a kitchen at baking time. Picking peas in the field, the students and teachers wore straw hats to shield their faces from the sun and perspired until their cotton shirts and dresses clung to them. They were there the day the dinner bell rang at three o'clock.

Jenny straightened and looked questioningly at Seth who worked near her. "What's that for?"

He stood and fanned his face with his hat. "It's not suppertime yet." Squinting at the sun, he said, "Maybe they want us to come in for something."

They started for the dining room. From across the field the others came—old hands like Meg and Rob, new ones like Leah Paton and Claire and Mary Lou Henderson. With questioning faces they entered. The professor waited for them. "All of you, sit down," he directed.

They sat down.

"We have a matter for special prayer this afternoon," he began. The room was quiet except for the kitchen clock's loud ticking. "The army worms are coming."

Scanning the serious young faces around her, Jenny thought they looked as puzzled as she felt.

"Maybe you've never seen them," Brannon went on, "but they're woolly, brown worms about the size of your finger, called 'army worms' because they come in large numbers and eat every green thing in their path." Jenny gasped. She thought of her sack of freshly picked peas lying in the field. "The way they're coming, they should reach us sometime tomorrow. Do you know what that would mean?"

No one spoke. At the back of the room Mrs. Grant shook her head slowly.

"We have to work hard to keep food on the table," the professor explained solemnly. "We just can't afford to lose our crops."

Still no one said anything. It seemed to Jenny that her home and her longed-for Christian education were suddenly in danger. She swallowed hard.

"But we've tried to be faithful to God." Calmly Brannon picked up his Bible and opened it. "We've returned a tithe on our increase without fail, and now we must claim the promise." He began to read.

"Bring ye all the tithes into the storehouse . . . and prove me now herewith, saith the Lord of hosts, if I will not open you the windows of heaven, and pour you out a blessing. . . .

"And I will rebuke the devourer for your sakes, and he shall not destroy the fruits of your ground." *

The professor closed the Book. "Young people," he said, "let us kneel."

It was the strangest prayer meeting Jenny had ever attended—young men and women pleading with the Creator to "rebuke" the horde of woolly worms that chewed their way across Georgia.

The next afternoon at four o'clock the dinner bell rang again. In the field, Jenny dropped a handful of peas into her sack. Then without a word she began to run.

* Malachi 3:10, 11.

11

Panting, Jenny crowded through the dining room door alongside Leah and Meg.

"Let's thank God!" Professor Brannon exclaimed as they entered. "The army worms came as far as the ditch by the road yonder"—he pointed toward the dirt road bordering the school's farmland—"and *stayed* there."

"Thank the Lord!" Mrs. Grant murmured, clasping her large hands and breaking into a smile.

"I watched them struggle and roll into a heap about as big around as a man," the professor said, his face glowing, "but they couldn't seem to get out. Go see for yourself!"

Jenny was speechless. God knew about Flat Rock! He had heard their prayer, and He had kept His promise!

Eagerly Seth started for the door, but Brannon halted him. "First, young people," he said, "let us kneel!"

Letters from home were few but treasured. Effie's first child was a boy, Lil was expecting her second, and Pa was fine. Once in a while Bob sent Jenny a dollar. She reckoned her letters sounded strange to them, caught up as they were with family affairs. (She was ready for seventh grade . . . A new roommate was coming . . . A boy named Rob had put a dead skunk in her tent-house yard . . .)

When she looked into the long mirror at Meg's house, Jenny saw a woman reflected there, yet she still delighted in girlish fun. It was as though, for her, girlhood had come around late. She wondered why, when a person was happy, the time went by fast, and why, when a girl passed 20, the years gained speed? Without a doubt they did, like the wheels of the farm wagon starting out slow and rolling faster and faster down the dirt road to the Dog River.

Jenny's new roommate was fair-skinned and curly-haired. The first night Laura shared the tent-house, Jenny waited for her to fall asleep, then slipped quietly from bed and lit the lantern. Holding it above the sleeping girl, she studied the childlike face and dark curls shining auburn in the light. "Not a day over 15," she judged.

Next morning she took the girl to breakfast. "This is Laura," she told Claire and Mary Lou at the table. "She's from Valdosta, down in south Georgia."

Valdosta. The name sounded aristocratic to Jenny's ear. What kind of home did Laura come from? Would she turn up her nose at corn bread made with molasses? Jenny watched from the corner of her eye as the new roommate took a slab, crumbled it, and spooned cream gravy over it. Then she waited while her new roommate took a bite.

"Um-m-m!" Laura exclaimed. "This is mighty good!"

Grinning, Jenny reckoned she and the girl would get along.

School days blended one into the other, the chill of autumn deepening into winter, and winter easing into spring. Tim offered to give Jenny piano lessons free, and Seth took to leaving an onion beside her plate, learning that she loved them.

"They're your age," Meg commented with a wise nod. "The schoolboys are too young for you."

Jenny sighed. There was something to it, her being 21 in the seventh grade. She pictured Tim's suntanned face at the kitchen door as he tipped his straw hat and stomped earth from his boots—and Seth, his large frame resting on a cotton sack as he picked near her in the field. His voice was kind and his eyes honest. She liked Seth—and Tim, too. Still . . . .

She shook her head.

"Takes more than age to make a person 'just right,' " she

observed, unsure just what it did take.

Summer came on. A packinghouse in Atlanta gave their "cull" peaches to the little school near Douglasville. "What a blessing!" the professor exclaimed as he unloaded them from the farm wagon. "The Lord always provides!"

Jenny peeled peaches until her hand ached from gripping the knife. Her blouse clung to her back, and her hair to her damp forehead. "Maybe they *are* a blessing," she mused, rubbing her nose with the back of her hand. Peach juice dripped from her elbow. "But I'll be proud to finish with this peach fuzz!"

Hardly had the jars of yellow fruit cooled in the storeroom when the farm wagon arrived with a different sort of load.

"Give me a hand, Seth!" Mr. Brannon called as he unloaded horns, drums, and other musical instruments in front of the schoolhouse. Wordlessly Jenny watched the two men carry them inside.

"Where'd you get those, Professor?" she asked when he came out to take the wagon to the barn.

He hoisted himself into the driver's seat and grinned down at her. "Wouldn't you like to know!"

"I'm dying to!"

"All right. I'll tell you. A brass band in Atlanta went broke—and gave us all their instruments!"

Jenny shook her head in amazement. "I declare!"

"The Lord has blessed us again." The professor's grin grew even broader. "Now Flat Rock can have its own band."

"I reckon so."

"And put on programs and—" The man looked closely at her. *"You'd* like to be in the band, wouldn't you?"

"Oh—oh, yes!" Looking up at him, Jenny knew that the love of music ran in her veins. Once, she had enjoyed Ma and Pa and the neighbors' singing on the front porch on summer evenings, and Rosie Smith's playing the pump organ at church. But those things had only stirred the love that was there—*born* there—to be used.

"A teacher from Atlanta will give the lessons," Brannon

explained, smiling at her eager face. "Once a week for a dollar apiece."

In class that afternoon Jenny dreamed of a big horn, and as she pictured the sun glinting on its bell, she felt the rhythm of "Dixie" in her feet.

But the money! The thought of it came like a period at the end of a sentence or the turning of a key in a lock. Why, even if Bob should send her $5—and, of course, he would not . . . Jenny chewed the top of her penny pencil and pretended to puzzle over an arithmetic problem.

That evening after worship she waited for the others to leave before she spoke to the professor. "I'd like to play one of those big horns that sit on your lap," she said.

He nodded. "I see."

"But I don't know how I can." Jenny wished she could explain that finding a way to pay for things had to come first for her—like picking up stones from the cotton field before turning the ground or cutting brown spots from peaches before packing them in jars.

"You'd like lessons, but you don't have the money."

"Yes, sir."

"I've been thinking about that myself." Brannon pursed his lips and frowned. "There must be some way—"

"Professor," Jenny interrupted hopefully, "do you reckon there's any way a girl could earn a dollar a week cash?"

The man stroked his chin. "I'll see what I can think of, Jenny. Meantime, don't you fret about it."

Before the school had gathered the last of its cotton crop and laid out its sweet potatoes to cure on the storeroom floor, Jenny arrived at the tent-house one afternoon to find a new dress on her bed. Large-eyed, she read the note pinned to the front.

"To our girl with love, from Mrs. Brannon."

She picked up the dark-blue cotton and fingered the neat collar and the row of buttons down the front. Her throat tightened. Nobody had made her a dress since Ma.

" 'When my father and my mother forsake me, then the Lord will take me up,' " she said to herself.

Besides spelling, English, and arithmetic, Jenny took Seth's Bible course that school year. Seth was a good teacher, though she chuckled at the way he pointed with his thumb and little finger for emphasis, and blushed when he looked too long at her.

Night after night she pored over the textbook with its quaint pictures and its stories of Jesus. *The Desire of Ages.* She pondered its name. "That must mean that everybody—all through the years—has needed Him." Somehow she found it easier to memorize passages from that book than to learn spelling words. As if it meant more to her. As if that lonely Man of Sorrows was, in a special way, her Friend.

"Here's a good thought," she told Laura one evening, glancing up from her reading. "Listen. 'At all times and in all places, in all sorrows and in all afflictions, when the outlook seems dark and the future perplexing, and we feel helpless and alone, the Comforter will be sent in answer to the prayer of faith.' " *

"That's beautiful," her roommate agreed. "The Comforter—that's the Holy Spirit, isn't it?"

"Uh-huh." Jenny crossed her ankles and sat Indian-style on her patchwork quilt. Light from the lantern flickered on the pages of the book in her lap. "You know, these stories make the life of Christ plumb real! Bible is hard for me—prophecies and all—but this book . . . "

"It helps you understand the Bible."

"Yeah, that's it." She tucked her long nightgown snugly under her toes. "I reckon that's what it does."

When Professor Brannon called Jenny aside after worship one evening, she watched his face closely. Usually she could tell when he had good news. Sure enough, his eyes twinkled.

"How are you at ironing shirts?" he inquired.

"Fair, I reckon," she answered. "I commenced ironing

* Ellen G. White, *The Desire of Ages*, p. 669.

Pa's Sunday shirts when I was 13. Before that, Ma did it."

"I see." Brannon stroked his chin and cocked his head slightly. "You know, somebody has to iron the boys' shirts."

"You mean—"

"I mean for 10 cents apiece, *you* could."

"You mean—"

"Ten cents *cash.*"

Jenny smiled broadly.

"Yes, sir! I could do that!" she said. All the way to the tent-house she hummed "Dixie."

In all it was a fine school year, though illness claimed a part of it. First she had vague chills and fever, then a definite pain.

"Appears to me like the appendix," the doctor from Douglasville stated after probing to his satisfaction. He snapped his black bag shut and sent for a surgeon in Atlanta.

The whole thing was over in less than a week—the fearing, the drifting off to sleep on a table in the bathroom she and Effie had shared years before, and the waking up with sunlight streaming through the window.

"I'm mighty near good as new," Jenny told Leah and Meg as they climbed the slope to the schoolhouse one January day. "See the roses in my cheeks?"

Meg said disdainfully, "You've been pinching them."

"No, I haven't."

"Then it's love," Leah offered.

Jenny laughed. "Not that, either. Just the bloom of youth."

Seth looked up from his book as the three entered the classroom, giggling. He shook his head, but his eyes rested kindly on Jenny.

Later that week she found a package with a note reading "From Seth" on her bed. That same day Leah and Meg also got packages from him—new cotton stockings for each.

Jenny blushed to tell them that hers were silk.

12 Spring broke through winter at last, the green tips of daffodils poking up beside the path to the schoolhouse, and the trees across the pasture putting out young leaves. On Sundays the Flat Rock Band played on the grass by Dog River. It was marvelous. As the community folks clapped and cheered, Jenny felt her face warm with more than spring sunshine.

At the graduation ceremony in May, Seth awarded her a leather-bound *Desire of Ages*. "Lovingly presented to Jenny Thompson," read his careful inscription on the flyleaf. "Prize for leading the class in memorizing passages."

Alone in the tent-house, Jenny fingered the book's supple binding and read the words again. A little smile turned up the corners of her mouth. "Not bad for a cotton field girl!" she said aloud.

That summer she went to Bob's for a week. Again he took her in his wagon to see relatives—Lil and her growing family; Effie with her two towheads; Pa, again at Effie's place after spending time with his older daughters. He and Jenny chatted about Fillman's new calf and the cotton coming up in the field next to the square wooden farmhouse. He seemed pleased to see Jenny again, and she felt proud of that.

Back at Flat Rock she worried about the future. The picture of Lil and Effie making biscuits for their husbands and mothering their toddlers stayed with her. They had found their place in life. Where was hers?

"Seth is a good Christian man, Jenny," Professor Brannon observed knowingly as he chanced by the kitchen one morning. He seemed to peer right through her as she scrubbed intently at the gravy pan. "You could do a heap worse!"

"Yes, sir." She could not argue the point. Seth was a good Christian and a good friend, too. How could she explain to the professor that, in spite of all that, she did not love Seth? It was easier to tell Meg as they strolled barefoot toward the flat rock in the late afternoon.

"I like Seth"—Jenny tucked a vagrant brown curl behind her ear—"but I can't get serious with him, Meg."

The Brannon girl shook her head slowly. "He's stuck on you, Jenny. I can tell by the way he looks at you. Maybe he'd wait for you to finish school."

"It's not that."

"What is it then? Seth's mighty nice."

"I know. But I only *like* him—you know?" Jenny searched her friend's face for understanding.

Picking a blade of pasture grass, Meg twirled it between her palms. "You're plumb certain?"

"Plumb certain."

"All right." Meg tore the blade of grass down the middle and threw away the pieces. "You don't have to go with Seth, but mind you play fair with him."

"Well, of course," Jenny said. "I aim to."

How autumn followed autumn and school years marched by like days, Jenny could never tell. Hardly had old students finished tenth grade and gone away than new ones gathered around the white-oilcloth tables in the dining room.

"We're supposed to go out together today," Leah whispered to her one mild September morning as the students gathered for instructions before a missionary jaunt into the countryside. "I'm glad, because I don't know what to say to folks, and you do."

"Me?" Jenny smiled. "I guess I do talk right smart. I

found out if you're friendly, other folks generally are too."

Leah shook her head. "Sounds easy," she admitted, "but when I knock on a door . . ."

"I know. I'm a little bashful myself. But, with that beautiful long hair of yours, how could you be bashful?"

Leah's plump face lighted. "I'm still glad I'm with you."

They walked briskly at first, but slower as they neared the house indicated on the professor's hand-drawn map. "Yonder it is." Leah pointed as they rounded a bend. "One room and a lean-to."

Jenny stared at the small home perched on rock pillars, her eyes taking in the weathered wood, the rotting porch, the chickens pecking in the dirt yard. "You mean 'shanty.' " She thought fleetingly of the log house at home. It was weathered too, but bigger, and her family had kept it up.

As they neared the house they walked even slower.

"You do the talking, Jenny."

The children in the doorway did not take their eyes off the girls as they turned into the yard. "Hey there!" Jenny called brightly. "Your ma home?"

"In there," the taller of the two mumbled shyly, gesturing.

Trying to ignore the smell of old food and grease in the kitchen lean-to, Jenny moved toward the bed where a woman lay on dirty newspapers, a newborn child beside her. "Howdy, ma'am." She bent over the woman, motioning the other girl closer. "I'm Jenny, and this is Leah. We're from Flat Rock school. Reckon we could do something to make you easier?"

The woman's voice was soft, and when she looked up, her eyes reminded Jenny of a helpless animal. "Be proud if you would."

Leah looked questioningly at her roommate. "Shall I get the lady some clean shee—newspapers?"

"Yes, and help her wash up a speck. I'll mind the young ones."

The air outdoors was fresh and sweet smelling. Jenny took a deep breath. "What's your name, sister?" she asked the older child.

"Cora." The girl squiggled her toes in the dirt.

"That's a pretty name. What's your brother's name?"

"George." Cora spoke for the large-eyed child with a dirty thumb in his mouth.

Jenny studied the grimy little bodies, the soiled clothes, and the matted hair. Suddenly her eyes brightened. "Guess what, Cora and George!"

"What?" Cora said.

"We're going to give you a bath and wash your hair!"

Walking home, the girls chatted happily, scarcely aware of their tiredness.

"Her name's Mrs. Pilgrim, I found out," Leah said. "She can't be much older than you, poor soul."

"I know." Silence for a time, then Jenny chuckled. "Guess what I used to scrub the young ones' heads!"

"Water, I suppose."

"Nope."

"What, then?"

"Water to rinse, of course." Jenny laughed delightedly. "To scour—just plain old sand!"

Christmas at Flat Rock was never fancy, but the stars were as close as those over Bethlehem's hills, and the little pines in the woods as spicy as the tinseled trees of Atlanta.

In the dining room, everyone who had not gone home for the holiday gathered around the piano, and Tim sat on the swivel stool. Nearest him were Laura, Meg, and Jenny, with the professor and his wife close behind. Seth stood at the edge of the group beside newcomer Ben Black and his sister Sarah.

"How about 'Silent Night,' Tim?" Professor Brannon suggested. They all found their notes from Tim's chord, and music filled the room, plain as it was, with celebration.

"The stable wasn't fancy either," Jenny mused, glancing from one beaming face to another. "It didn't need to be."

76

"Angels are no farther from us now than they were from the shepherds," the professor remarked when the room was quiet. He pulled a chair from a table and seated himself.

"It's hard to remember that when you can't see them," Jenny offered, scooting her chair into the circle that was forming. "Seems like it's hard to believe things you can't see."

"Yeah," Meg agreed.

Even Brannon's wife nodded. "I reckon we'd worry less if we could see them."

"Or believe in them enough," the professor added. "You know, I like the story of Abraham taking angels home to dinner, not knowing who they were!" He chuckled softly.

Meg's eyes sparkled. "Wish *I* could see an angel!"

"Maybe you will, my dear." The professor looked fondly at his nearly grown daughter. " 'Be not forgetful to entertain strangers,' the Good Book says, 'for thereby some have entertained angels unawares.' " * He leaned forward confidentially. "I think sometimes they still appear in human form."

"You do?" Jenny studied the professor's face.

He nodded. "They may enter our lives more than we guess."

In the stillness the kitchen clock ticked loudly. "I think I may have seen one," Jenny said.

Everyone's eyes turned toward her.

"You do?" Even the professor looked surprised.

"Yes, sir, but I'm not sure."

"When, Jenny?" Meg asked incredulously.

"The day Effie and I came to Flat Rock. On our way from the train station—"

"That young man!" Meg interrupted. "Why, Jenny, it could have been!"

"I know it," Jenny replied. "I can't say for certain, but I reckon I'll always wonder."

February wind whipped at the oaks and whistled around the corner of the kitchen as Jenny lifted pans of fresh bread

* Hebrews 13:2.

77

from the oven and brushed their tops with cream. "Maybe I'm not the best in spelling," she remarked to Laura who worked nearby, "but I make about the best light bread!" She lifted a brown loaf to her nose.

"I don't doubt you do!" Laura flashed her a smile and turned to scouring sweet potatoes with a brush. "Now me—my talent is—"

"Scrubbing potatoes!" Jenny finished, laughing. She lined the loaves up evenly. "Thirty-seven, thirty-eight, thirty-nine, forty. Enough for the school and customers in Douglasville." Taking off her flour-sack apron, she hung it on a peg and slipped into her brown coat. Suddenly she turned to her roommate. "Did you see who Seth's been sitting with at breakfast?"

"Couldn't miss it. Three mornings in a row!"

"Sarah's a right nice girl. Think it's a match?"

"Might be. Hey, what happened to you and Seth?"

Jenny forced a laugh. "I'm not the marrying kind, I reckon."

Laura's blue eyes sparkled. "You just haven't found the right one yet."

"At 23, reckon I ever will?"

"Bound to—with that curly hair and those blue eyes!"

Jenny did not smile. "Maybe. But I'll tell you what. If I *don't*—she stood straight and spoke with a confidence that surprised herself—"there are things a heap worse than being single!" Pushing the door open, she stepped into the wind.

13 On the first day of April, Jenny and Leah received a note written in small, uncertain letters. It read:

"To the girls who helped out after the young one was born. Please come to dinner on Sunday. Twelve o'clock. From Millie Pilgrim."

They went. Seated at a small table in the lean-to, they chatted with Millie, her husband Jim, and the children whose faces were scrubbed to the hairline.

"I knew what you were thinking, Leah," Jenny confided as they walked back to Flat Rock that afternoon. "If there were germs, you hoped we'd be spared!"

The other girl tossed her long hair and laughed. "How'd you know?"

"Well, what do you think *I* was thinking?" Jenny laughed too. Then she sobered. "But she did the best she could. She didn't have much to do with. If the chickens hadn't already laid, we wouldn't have had anything to eat."

"You're right. We wouldn't have."

"What a brave little soul!"

"Yeah."

The sun was still high when they came in view of Flat Rock with its blue frame schoolhouse crowning the hillside. Under the oaks the grass was shade-dappled, but spring rains had brightened it. Like a carpet it covered the slope, and above, the sky was splendid. It seemed the kind of day for making plans.

"When I finish here," Jenny spoke her thoughts aloud,

"I think I want to . . ."

"What?" Leah strode to keep up, puffing a little.

"I want to work with people," she finished.

"You do?"

"Uh-huh." Jenny slowed her pace as though the idea required deep thought. "I don't know how yet, but I do like people—I know that."

Leah's eyes were admiring. "You have a talent. The Lord'll show you how to use it."

With spring and graduation on the schoolhouse lawn, Jenny felt something strange in the pit of her stomach. At first she could not define it, but at night, alone in the tent-house, she knew just what it was. Next May when the professor handed out certificates, she—Jenny Thompson—would be leaving Flat Rock.

She stood at the window for a long time, recalling the years since Ma died and she had first known what it was to feel alone. Now she grappled with the thought that one more cycle of seasons would tear another home, another family from her.

How could she leave this place? Where would she go? Not to the flatwoods, surely. There was nothing there for her. Not to Southern Junior College as much as she might wish to . . .

Among the oaks the tent-houses were dark. Not a bird stirred. Not even a cricket broke the stillness. She looked up at the quiet stars. "Where am I going?" she asked. But they held their peace.

The beginning of her last school year at Flat Rock was as exciting as every other, except that she felt less exuberant at 23 than 18. Life was like eating corn bread, she allowed. Though the second and third pieces were as good as the first, your appetite lost its zest. You ate because you were not yet full. And you ate to clean your plate.

Still she studied each newcomer with interest. At once she liked Alice Henton with the soft giggle. Toward the awkward and bashful new boys she had an almost motherly attitude.

One thing she disliked about new school years was the emptiness she felt for friends who did not return. It was always there—a little pang in the midst of happiness. This year she felt it for Seth.

"I'll have to be friendly to Sarah," she remarked to Meg as they left the dining room one evening. "She looks lost, with Seth gone off to teach somewhere else!" Turning to her friend, she asked, "Did you know Sarah's an orphan?"

"I heard that."

The girls strolled quietly toward the tent-house in the warm September evening. After a time Jenny spoke. "I reckon there are lots of lonely folks we don't know about."

"Yeah, and folks with nobody to care."

Again the two walked in silence. As they reached the tent-house, the sun went behind the trees, and the air was suddenly cool.

"You know what, Jenny?" Meg spoke fervently. "We're mighty lucky!"

"I know it," she said softly.

Besides new students, Flat Rock had a new kitchen matron that year—a round-faced little woman who approached Jenny right off.

"I'm Miz Dayton," she introduced herself, propelling the girl toward a basket of late peas. "Pull up a chair beside me."

Jenny scooted her chair close to the basket and took the pan the woman handed her.

" You can call me 'Ma Dayton,' " the woman went on, studying the younger woman with bright blue eyes. "I like to be a kind of 'mother' to young ones away at school, you know. Sounds better than plain old 'Miz' anyway, doesn't it?" She chatted on. Jenny did not dislike the friendly new matron, yet she felt uneasy. Shelling silently, she fell to watching her hands and the little speckled peas that slid into her pan. At last she had to speak.

"Miz Dayton," she began, staring the woman straight in

the eye, "I don't reckon I'll be calling you 'Ma' like the rest."

The matron looked surprised. "Oh? Why not?"

Jenny examined four peas lined up neatly in the green pod in her hand. "I had only one ma," she said quietly. "And she's dead. I don't aim to call anybody else that." She raised her eyes again to the woman's face. "But I'll like you fine just the same."

Mrs. Dayton reached over and patted her knee. "Go ahead and call me 'Miz Dayton' if you want to," she said kindly. "But it's OK if you change your mind."

"Thank you, ma'am," Jenny said, knowing that she would not.

The months passed too fast, blue and gold autumn giving way to a winter that blanketed the campus twice with snow.

"I don't know where I'll go when school's out," she wrote to Effie in a short, easy sentence that gave no hint of the hours she lay awake, wondering.

"I could go live with my sister," she told Mrs. Dayton as they scrubbed potatoes for boiling. "But she's got her own family . . ."

The matron listened quietly. "H'mm," she said, frowning. "Jenny, you let me think awhile. Maybe I can come up with something. The good Lord's led you this far for some reason." Suddenly her face changed, as though she thought of something else. "By the way, I've been having right smart trouble with my back of late. If I paid you a pair of new stockings, reckon you could give me some hot packs tonight?"

Trying not to glance at the mended spot in her stocking, she answered, "Why, sure, Miz Dayton. I'd be proud to."

In late February Jenny still had no plans for the future. She tried to study and chat with the other students as usual, but she found herself falling silent, and noticed that often the words in her textbooks blurred. Only at worship could she feel the grip of her fear lessen.

" 'Those who accept Christ as their personal Saviour are not left as orphans . . .' " Professor Brannon read one evening from his well-marked *Desire of Ages*. " 'He bids them call His Father their Father. They are His "little ones," dear to the heart of God.' " *

Twilight now came early, and through the dining room window the first stars shone soft and faint.

"Will you play for us, Tim?" The professor gestured toward the piano. Tim struck the chord, and the students sang without songbooks.

"All the way my Saviour leads me; What have I to ask beside? . . ."

Walking to the tent-house afterward, Jenny hummed the song. When she looked up, the sky was almost black, and the stars seemed bright and near. "My Father is right up there," she said to herself.

March passed, and half of April. Jenny observed that Sarah heard from Seth regularly as summer approached. On the pasture fence, bluebirds talked softly of nesting spots, and even in Jenny's bones there seemed a restlessness—for what, she could not tell.

"Is it almost warm enough to slide down the flat rock?" she wondered aloud as she and Alice set the tables for dinner.

"Sounds like spring fever!" Alice diagnosed, her eyes merry. "But have you felt the breeze? It's plumb chilly!"

Jenny sniffed. "Practical Alice," she said with a shake of her curls. "You'd test the water with a thermometer!"

The two were laughing when Mrs. Dayton bustled into the dining room, freshly aproned for the noon meal. "Looks right nice, girls!" She winked at Jenny, then lowered her voice. "I spoke to my husband about you, and he has an idea!" With that she hurried off to ring the dinner bell.

* White, *The Desire of Ages*, p. 327.

14 Art Dayton ("Brother Dayton," the students called him) was a slender man, thin-faced and balding. Seeing how he walked with a spring in his step, Jenny did not wonder that he supervised the selling of Christian books door to door.

"What'd your husband say, Miz Dayton?" she ventured that evening, lingering after the other help left the kitchen.

The little woman stacked the last of the bowls in the cupboard. "Appears to be a need for somebody to sell books in Atlanta," she said crisply, hanging her dish towel to dry. "Like to try?"

"*Me?*" Jenny stood still for a moment, letting the words seep into her mind. Like rain running off red clay by any gully it could find, the thought soaked in slowly.

"Why, yes. Why not?"

"Well, I—Where would I stay?"

"There's a Miz Becker lives right near the church in Atlanta. She and her daughter Martha would be proud to take you in."

"I—I don't know—" Jenny shook her head. "I've never—"

"You study about it." Mrs. Dayton smiled as she reached for her ring of house keys. "Art'll be glad to talk to you."

"Yes, ma'am." The two stepped out of the dining room into the April evening. "I'll let you know soon as I can." Jenny took a roundabout way to the tent-house, walking slowly and alone.

Afternoon shadows reached out from the oaks and tent-houses on the slope, and the breeze was almost warm. Jenny leaned against a rough tree trunk and stared at the English book in her lap.

" 'The conductor stepped quickly . . . ' " she mumbled, furrowing her forehead. "Are you good at nouns, Meg?"

The Brannon girl glanced up from her book.

"Nouns? Oh, fair. But I'm tired of studying!" She snapped the book shut. "Smell that plowed field yonder! Do you realize there's just one more week of school?"

Jenny closed her book and fingered an acorn on the ground. "I can hardly believe it." Her voice was flat.

Meg noticed. "Homesick already?" she questioned.

"Maybe," Jenny said after a forced laugh.

"Well"—Meg straightened her shoulders and assumed her wisest look—"let's think of it this way. You aren't going to China, only Atlanta, and it's not *that* far away!"

"Keep talking, Meg! And tell me I can sell books!"

"You can sell books," Meg said, and both girls laughed lightheartedly.

On graduation morning sparrows chirped happily around the eaves of the schoolhouse, and on the grass, rows of chairs filled quickly.

From her front-row seat Jenny looked across the pasture toward the woods, lacy with light-green leaves. Yonder was the spring, the hollow tree, the flat rock . . . and here, the freshly planted earth, the tent-houses, the dining room door at which she stood six years ago. A lump rose in her throat. She had *lived* so much in this place!

But she must not cry. Taking a deep breath, she fixed her mind on the ceremony.

"Young people, as you leave this school where we have worked, studied, and prayed together . . ." It was no use. The professor's words faded and his gray suit blurred. How she loved that man! It seemed to her that the heavenly Father must be something like him.

Suddenly it was time for the graduates to walk to the

front for their certificates. Laura. Leah. Then Jenny's turn.

Six years could not fit on a piece of paper or be recalled in a moment. As she reached for her certificate, she did not feel the sense of high achievement she had imagined, only a comfortable satisfaction that mingled strangely with the sadness of parting.

"Congratulations, Jenny!" His eyes twinkling, the professor grasped her free hand in his rough one.

"Thank you, sir."

It was all over. Now she knew she must smile—or dissolve into tears in front of everyone. She smiled widely—smiled all the way to her seat.

Jenny did not look at Meg or the professor and his wife as she walked from them to the Model T in front of the dining room. At the car Mrs. Dayton handed her a little sack.

"Here's some lunch for the two of you," she said. "See that Art drives carefully."

"I'll look out for him," Jenny promised. She glanced over the woman's shoulder. " 'Bye, Meg."

"Be good, Jenny."

"You too."

Mr. Dayton lifted her suitcase into the back of the car, turned the crank, and jumped behind the steering wheel. A chug, a rattle, and a lurch, and they were off.

"Right nice little ride into Atlanta," Mr. Dayton said after a while. "Once you get there, streets are paved. You'll even have sidewalks."

Jenny blew her nose. "That so?"

"And streetlights," the man went on. "But you'd best stay inside nights. Not safe, you know."

"Yes, sir." She nodded appropriately, having never lived where you couldn't walk under the stars if you wanted to.

"But you'll like it, once you get acquainted. Miz Becker and Martha are fine people."

"Yes, sir."

The countryside bobbed past. Looking out at cotton

fields and peach orchards, Jenny did not say much. Her head filled with sidewalks, streetlights, and rows of city houses where people waited to buy books.

Mrs. Becker was a fine person, plump and gray-haired with the wrinkles of seventy summers in her cheeks.

"Here's your bed, dearie," she said, showing her to the couch in the first-floor hallway of her two-story frame house. "There's a spot yonder for your suitcase and a peg for your clothes. There's more room for hanging things in the bedroom"—she glanced at Jenny's one suitcase—"if you need it."

"This'll be fine." Spreading open her suitcase, Jenny took out the middy suit and the blue dress the professor's wife had made. She hung them on the peg. "Now there," she said. "We're all settled."

"You're going to do all right, dearie." Mrs. Becker patted her boarder's shoulder. "Must be many a soul out there needs what you have to sell!"

At 50, Martha was quieter than her mother but just as good-hearted, Jenny judged. "Here's an extra cover," the younger woman said, appearing in the doorway with a light quilt over her arm. "Most nights you won't need it, but it can turn off cool."

After she was alone, Jenny surveyed her living quarters. The velvety-covered old couch was the only piece of furniture in the hallway. From the wooden floor to the bare electric light bulb at the ceiling, everything was plain except the wallpaper. It was white with fragile blue and pink patterns.

"A bathroom to sleep in at Flat Rock—and now a hall," she mused. "But that's all right. I can 'rough it.' I always have."

The sun was up a good way when Jenny left the Becker home in the morning, clutching a small satchel Mr. Dayton had given her. Straightening her shoulders, she thought of the twenty little books inside—ten of *The Other Side of Death* and ten of *The Second Coming*. Though they cost only 25 cents apiece, she knew they were valuable. Why, what would she have done without the hope between their covers?

The sidewalk stretched long and straight, and she walked six blocks before stopping in front of a white house with shrubs around the porch.

"You have a talent, Jenny," Leah had told her.

"I want to work with people." She had said that herself. Well, here she was.

Trying to look confident, she walked up to the door. For a moment she stood there, her heart racing. Twice she raised her hand to knock and let it fall.

"Help me, Lord!" she prayed. Then she finally knocked. The door opened into an entryway with a long mirror at the back. Stiffly Jenny smiled at the sleepy-eyed woman in robe and slippers.

"Pardon me, ma'am. I'm sorry to—"

"Yes?" The woman did not smile.

"I—uh— Do you—"

The woman looked at the satchel. "If you're selling something, I'm not interested." She began closing the door.

Jenny's smile stiffened more. "Thank you anyway."

As the sun climbed high over the three-story buildings on Peachtree Street, and the streets teemed with buggies, wagons, and Model T's, she sat in a strange park to rest. Perspiration wet the back of her middy blouse. Her feet ached.

"Maybe I'll sell some here," she encouraged herself, starting down another long sidewalk. "Judging by the houses, the folks on this street are well-to-do."

But the man in the brick house had lost his job, and the one in the white two-story was retired. No one was at home in the house with pillars. The mother in the yellow frame one was in the hospital.

"It's all right," Jenny sympathized over and over. "I

know just how it is!"

Shooing flies with one hand, Mrs. Becker opened the screen door for Jenny. Questions lurked in her eyes, but she did not ask them. "Well, dearie, you must be tired!" was all she said.

"Yes, ma'am." One more time Jenny tried to smile before going to her hall.

Pulling off her shoes, she stretched out on the couch and wiggled her toes. Then she lay limp until the tiredness drained from her body.

"My, my!" she marveled as her eyes wandered over the dainty blue and pink figures on the wallpaper. "There are a heap more poor people than I ever reckoned there were!"

15 For two weeks Jenny trudged the streets of Atlanta, on good days selling two or three books, and on bad ones nothing at all. Little varied her schedule. Once in a while Mr. Dayton stopped by. Sometimes she walked to prayer meeting with Mrs. Becker and Martha, but most evenings she simply went to her hall, where, weary as she was, she often lay awake for a long time.

She could not sell. The fact settled on her mind lightly at first, then heavy as a satchel full of books. Having come to Atlanta thinking it was meant to be, she'd tried to be diligent. What had happened?

"All the way my Saviour leads me;
What have I to ask beside?"

Almost she could hear the students at Flat Rock singing and see the professor's kind face, glowing with his faith. It was easier to have faith at Flat Rock.

On her couch in the dark hallway, Jenny pulled the quilt over her and buried her face in the pillow. "Lord, if You're still leading me, please—show me what to do!" Tears fell on the pillow, and finally she slept.

The third week began much like the other two, though the soles of her shoes were thinner. As her feet measured the distance between houses, she let her mind run free.

Strange how the thought of Southern Junior College came to her now and again, like a song months after she'd heard it, or a memory returning after years.

"Reckon how it would be to go to school in Tennessee?" she wondered. "Reckon what you'd learn there?"

She had no way to know. Even if she could work her way at Southern Junior—as she began to hope she could—she had no way of getting there. Suddenly Jenny felt like a cotton field girl, straightening beside her hoe and looking away toward the hill . . .

Wednesday morning was bright and warm. Mrs. Becker opened the kitchen door to let out the heat from the cookstove.

"If you can come home a speck early tonight"—the woman dabbed at her damp forehead with her apron—"you and me and Martha'll go to prayer meeting."

Jenny swallowed a last bite of grits and gravy.

"Might as well, I reckon. No use working late." She left it at that, not wishing to bare her heart to her new friends, kind as they were.

"I could go back to Flat Rock," she mused, starting down the sidewalk. "Brother Dayton would take me there, and Miz Dayton would teach me to be a matron." She toyed with the idea of leaving unfamiliar streets and faces and getting her hands in the bread dough back at Flat Rock. It appealed to her—yet something was missing.

Why had she left Flat Rock anyway? Was it only because she had finished tenth grade?

She shifted the satchel from one hand to the other. "Funny," she said to herself idly, slowing under a maple that overhung the sidewalk, "how I've always wanted to make something of myself." She paused in the shade, tracing a sidewalk leaf shadow with her shoe. "Funny how I still have that feeling."

Worshiping in the Atlanta church was different from drawing chairs into a semicircle at Flat Rock. Rows of polished pews flanked a long aisle. Through high western windows sunlight streamed in on the mostly gray heads gathered midweek to pray. Yet there was something the same—Jenny noticed it right off. The friendship! It spoke to her rootlessness.

"Why, Christians are a family!" she said to herself, sharing her *Christ in Song* hymnbook with Martha and singing so lustily that others turned to look.

They had finished prayer and were partway through the preacher's talk when she felt a tap on her shoulder. Turning, she nearly bumped into the white envelope a sweet-faced old lady thrust toward her.

"For me?" She raised her eyebrows.

The woman nodded.

Jenny took the envelope and held it in her lap. What was it? She did not know anybody here except Mrs. Becker and Martha. Frowning, she stared at the unfamiliar handwriting on the envelope.

"To the girl . . . " She blinked and read the words again. "To the girl who is going to school." Inside the envelope was no letter, only a $10 bill.

The rest of the preacher's words floated over her like clouds blowing away from Atlanta. *To the girl who is going to school!* "Thank You, Lord," she said, bowing her head. "I take this for my answer."

With five dollars Jenny bought a new middy dress, and with five a ticket to Ooltewah, Tennessee. It was all she needed.

"I reckon I'll never know who gave it to me," she remarked to Mr. Dayton on the way to the train station. "But it makes me feel like they'll take me in at Southern Junior. It seems like the Lord is showing me the way."

Dayton nodded thoughtfully. "I don't doubt He is."

On the platform people milled about—idling, hurrying, bumping, pushing. Jenny did not know when she had seen so many. The little station at Douglasville was nothing like this. Her ticket grew damp in her hand.

"Ooltewah," she read the word stamped on it. It looked strange.

On a nearby track, a black train hissed to a stop, people got off, and strangers hugged other strangers. "That's your train," Mr. Dayton said. He set her suitcase beside her and held out his hand. It felt warm to her cold one.

"God bless you, Jenny."

"Goodbye, Brother Dayton."

The conductor reached for her ticket.

"Ooltewah," he said, punching it hurriedly, as though every day people went to places with strange names, as though every day they went where they had never been and nobody knew they were coming.

For a moment, aloneness almost overcame her. It was like the day she sold Daisy, and Pa sold the beds and the biscuit pan. The conductor's hand at her elbow urged her onto the train steps, but she held back.

Could she *do* this?

"Seest thou a man diligent . . . ?" The old lantern flickered softly in the storm. *"He shall stand before kings."*

"Help with your bag, ma'am?" A porter tipped his red cap and reached toward her suitcase.

The girl nodded.

"That would be mighty nice." Squaring her shoulders and looking straight ahead, she placed her foot upon the first step.

EPILOGUE

Jenny Thompson spent two years at Southern Junior College before going to the Florida Sanitarium where she learned to give physiotherapy treatments to the sick.

Later at the Washington Sanitarium, she treated celebrities like Arthur Godfrey (a radio personality), Elder and Mrs. A. G. Daniells (president of the General Conference of Seventh-day Adventists and his wife), and United States Senators and their wives.

When she met wavy-haired insurance salesman Tim O'Neil, she did not guess that one day he would become a Seventh-day Adventist minister—and she, that minister's wife.

Looking back, perhaps Jenny would tell you that a poor girl is as important to the heavenly Father as anyone else, and that His promise is good for anybody who claims it.